SEE U IN YOU

PASSION, CAREER & PAISA

THE UNIQUE LIFE GUIDE WITH 21 ACTIVITIES

SEE U IN YOU

PASSION, CAREER & PAISA

THE UNIQUE LIFE GUIDE WITH 21 ACTIVITIES

Authored by

AKHILESH TELKAR

Author of

Find "U" in "YOU"

#finduinyou

PENMAN BOOKS
A BOOK PUBLISHING COMPANY

PENMAN BOOKS

Office No. 303, Kumar House Building
D Block, Central Market, Opp. PVR Cinema,
Prashant Vihar, Delhi 110085, India
Website: www.penmanbooks.com
Email: publish@penmanbooks.com

First Published by Penman Books 2023

Title: See "U" in "YOU" — Passion, Career & Paisa

ISBN: 978-81-962772-0-8

LIMITS OF LIABILITY/DISCLAIMER OF WARRANTY: The author and publisher of this book have used their best efforts in preparing this material. The author and publisher make no representation or warranties with respect to the accuracy, applicability or completeness of the contents. They disclaim any warranties (expressed or implied), or merchantability for any particular purpose. The author and publisher shall in no event be held liable for any loss or other damages, including but not limited to special, incidental, consequential, or other damages. The information presented in this publication is compiled from sources believed to be accurate, however, both the publisher and author assume no responsibility for errors or omissions. The information in this publication is not intended to replace or substitute professional advice. The strategies outlined in this book may not be suitable for every individual, and are not meant to provide individualized advice or recommendations.

The advice and strategies found within may not be suitable for every situation. This work is sold with the understanding that neither the author nor the publisher are held responsible for the results accrued from the advice in this book.

All disputes are subject to Delhi jurisdiction only.

Stop being Common
Be the best version of Yourself
Change the old belief in you
Find "U" in "YOU"
Find the Passion in You
Become unstoppable and transform your career
Ultimately, fill the success bag with Paisa
See "U" in "YOU"
"The Unique Life Guide with 21 Activities"

Warning: *50% of people who buy a self-help book won't read till the end, what about you?*

TABLE OF CONTENTS

DEDICATION

I dedicate this book to my mother, who has always been there for me; not only emotionally but also spiritually.

ದೇವರು ಇಲ್ಲದ ಗುಡಿ ಇಲ್ಲ ತಾಯಿಲ್ಲದ ಮನೆ ಇಲ್ಲ
ನೋವಿಲ್ಲದ ಜೀವನ ಇಲ್ಲ ಅಮ್ಮ ಇಲ್ಲದ ಬಾಳು ಖುಷಿ ಇಲ್ಲ, ಆ ಖುಷಿ ನಿನ್ ತಾನೇ 🙏

(No temple without God, No house without Mother, No life without pain, No happiness without mother, the Biggest reason for happiness is only you! - Mom)

ನಾ ಬರುವೆ ಎಂದು ಗೊತ್ತಾಗಿದ್ದಾಗ ನೋವಲ್ಲಿ ಖುಷಿ ಕಂಡಿದ್ದು, ಅದು ನೀನ್ ತಾನೇ,

(Even in the terrible delivery pain you were happy, because you knew I was coming to this world, it's only you! - Mom)

ನಾನು ಕಣ್ಣು ಬಿಟ್ಟಾಗ, ಅತ್ತಾಗ, ಖುಷಿಯಲ್ಲಿ ಕಣ್ಣೀರು ಹಾಕಿದ್ದು ,ಅದು ನೀನ್ ತಾನೇ,

(When I opened my eyes, when I cried for the first time, despite the thick film of tears in your eyes, you were still happy to see me, it's only you! - Mom)

ಹಸಿವು ಇಲ್ಲದಿದ್ದರೂ ಇಷ್ಟ ಇಲ್ಲದಿದ್ದರೂ ನನಗೋಸ್ಕರ ಆಹಾರ ಸೇವಿಸಿದ್ದು, ಅದು ನೀನ್ ತಾನೇ,

(Even if you were not hungry, even if you did not like the menu, you still savored healthy food so that I could get nutrition, it's only you! - Mom)

ದೇಹದ ಆಕಾರ ದೇಹದ ಚಿಂತನೆ ಇದ್ದರೂನು ಎಲ್ಲಾ ಸಹಿಸಿ ನನ್ನ ಬೆಳವಣಿಗೆ ಬಗ್ಗೆ ಚಿಂತನೆ ಮಾಡುತ್ತಿದ್ದು,ಅದು ನೀನ್ ತಾನೇ,

(You took pain to grow-up me, not bothering about your bodily changes because of delivery, still, you were always worried about my growth, it's only you! - Mom)

ನಾ ಮಲಗಲಿ ಅಂತ ನೀ ಮಲಗದೆ ಇದ್ದಿದ್ದು,ಅದು ನೀನ್ ತಾನೇ,

(You didn't sleep properly so that I could sleep, it's only you! - Mom)

ದಿನದ ಎಷ್ಟೇ ಪರಿಶ್ರಮ ಇರಲಿ ಎಷ್ಟೇ ದಣಿವು ಒಮ್ಮೆ ಅಮ್ಮ ಎಂದು ಕರೆದರೆ ಸಾಕು ಸದಾ ನನ್ನ ಬಳಿ ಚಿಕ್ಕ ಬೇಡಿಕೆಗೆ ಸದಾ ಸಿದ್ಧ ಇರುವುದು,ಅದು ನೀನ್ ತಾನೇ,

(Whatever the work you have, however tired you are, if I call just once "AMMA", you leave everything and come to me, it's only you! - Mom)

ದೇವರು ಇಲ್ಲದ ಗುಡಿ ಇಲ್ಲ ತಾಯಿಲ್ಲದ ಮನೆ ಇಲ್ಲ

ನೋವಿಲ್ಲದ ಜೀವನ ಇಲ್ಲ ಅಮ್ಮ ಇಲ್ಲದ ಬಾಳು ಖುಷಿ ಇಲ್ಲ, ಆ ಖುಷಿ ನಿನ್ ತಾನೇ 🙏

(No temple without God, No house without Mother)

No life without pain, No happiness without mother, the Biggest reason for happiness is only you! - Mom)

To the experts, my family, my teachers, my friends and the people who helped me to become who I am today. Many of you have had a huge impact on my life in battling with challenges in business, in career, and in relationships.

Thanks for your will to contribute so I could grow.

And to my amazing son, Atharva, who has given me a reason to make this world a better place. Your future is what drives me today.

My heartful thanks to Dr. Lokesh who runs Kaivalya. Through him, my spark toward self-development started.

I dedicate this book to Dev Gadhvi my Mentor, who has transformed me and helped me discover my passion. He reignited my career at a dark time when I had almost thrown in the towel. I am grateful that your inspiration gave me a second chance. I believe this book transforms millions of passionate, career-oriented people!

Thank you, Devguru!

PREFACE

"Every Human being on this earth has come for some Purpose; Know your Calling, Passion, and Reason for being here... If you know early in your life, this is the first step to 'Success'."

—Akhilesh Telkar

A palliative nurse who has counseled the dying in their last days has revealed the most common regrets we have at the end of our lives.

The top five regrets before we leave this world are:

- "I wish I had the courage to live a life true to myself, not the life others expected of me."
- "I wish I hadn't worked so hard."
- "I wish I had the courage to express my feelings."
- "I wish I had stayed in touch with my friends."
- "I wish I had let myself be happier."

Bronnie Ware is an Australian nurse who spent several years working in palliative care, caring for patients in the last 12 weeks of their lives. She recorded their dying epiphanies.

After reading this, I questioned myself:

1. What is the one thing I can give to this world before I Go…?

2. How can I transform people's lives so that I won't regret it during my last moments?

The initial phase of my career was full of struggles, as I had no clarity of which pathway to take. Gradually, my quest to add to the treasure trove of my learning and handle any situation burst the clouds of confusion. I decided to follow my passion, which sparked a marvelous discovery. And that is the formula of "Find "U" in "You". Therefore, I decided to share my learning and experience with beginners and already working professionals through this book.

I can say that I foster a blend of **"Passion and technical skill = Passiontech".**

In plain words, Seeing "U" in "YOU" means discovering yourself. And who can be the best support to help you explore yourself?

YOU!

Yes, it is you who can See "U" in "YOU" with the help of this book as your guiding torch.

Here are the 4 major challenges that most people encounter while on the journey of this self-discovery:

- ➤ Puzzling out who you are
- ➤ Decoding your potential
- ➤ Knowing your calling
- ➤ Building your character

"Don't just become a dreamer, take action,
Implement and become an Achiever."

— Akhilesh Telkar

There are times when we lose our focus in life. Especially at the onset of our career journey, we might pour over if we are on the right career path.

Let me share with you the 4 Powerful Ws.

1. Where to start?
2. Which path to go?
3. What next to do?
4. Whom to contact?

Finding an answer to these can navigate you to the right track:

1. What is my area of interest?
2. Which Type of rewards can I reap if I follow my passion (remuneration + fulfillment)?
3. Whom can I contact to seek guidance (on my chosen career path)?

The ideal way is to write these questions on paper and try to dig out the answers.

By the end of this book, you will get clarity about:

Passion : What you might have been ignoring so far.

Career : Build the career you are looking for.

Paisa : Followed by Vitamin M (Money). Who doesn't want this?

See "U" in "YOU" is as much about learning as it is about "unlearning"! You must recognize how your old ways of thinking and acting have got you where you are right now.

So, be change-ready!

Unless you don't commit to change, no tool or word of advice is going to inspire!

Pull gear up to re-program your old beliefs and see new avatars of you!

We all are seekers in this big blue marble. However, there is a rare breed of people who transform from a Seeker to a Giver. Whereas others remain a seeker forever. So, you may want to ask yourself: Are you here on this planet to be a **Seeker or a Giver?**

"Don't become everyone, Become
One from Everyone, Make happy Everyone."

— Akhilesh Telkar

You work hard,

But for someone else,

It's now time to change - begin working from inside,

Don't try to change others,

Start working towards yourself so that you can contribute to others,

Because what you become is much more valuable than what you are.

If not now, when?

Not Ready Yet

Not Ready Yet

Not Ready Yet

Duniya ka sab se khubsurat word - "Pyar"
P se shuru hota hai...
Duniya ka sab se khatarnak word - "Power"
P se shuru hota hai...
Duniya ka sabse zimmedaar wala word - "Parents"
P se shur hota hai...
Duniya ki sabse keemti cheez - "Pendant" (diamond)
P se shuru hota hai...
Duniya jinke esharon pe chalti hai - "President"
P se shuru hota hai...
Duniya ka aaj tak ka dangerous word - "Pandemic"
P se shuru hota hai...
Duniya mein aaj tak jo samaj se bahar hai - "Patni"...
P se shuru hota hai…
Duniya mein sabse bada lagaav - "Pariwar"
P se shuru hota hai…
Duniya mein sab log jo nahi chahate, lekin hai phir bhi aa jaati hai - "Pain"
P se shuru hota hai…
Duniya mein sabko pata hai, lekin ignore karte hai - "Passion"
P se shuru hota hai…
Duniya me sabko chahiye, lekin aasani se nahi mila tha hai - "Paisa"
P se shuru hota hai…
Duniya jise dhund rahi hai, duniya ke sabse bade-bade words like - "Purpose, Positive energy, Performers, Perfect Personality, Pioneers"

P se shuru hote hain

Ye sab kahan hai, pata hai? All this information is available in this book!

So P se shuru karo Padana,

Positive mind se.

FOREWORD

This page is dedicated to all the artists, authors and great leaders in this world.

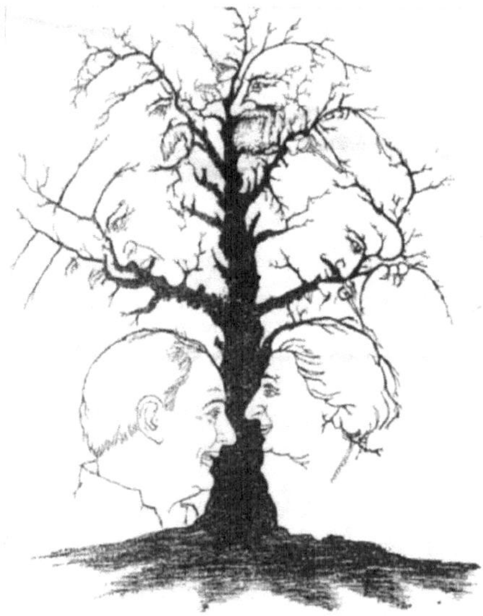

AUTHOR'S TREE

Can you find how many faces of famous personalities are there in this tree? Can you name them? (The answer is on the last page.)

The idea of this exercise is, there are a few elements that inspire us to be creative in every aspect of life.

1. Look at the beauty of art behind this innovative work. The artist not only drew a tree picture but also crafted our great leaders' faces in it.
2. So, let's be creative like this tree and appreciate the artist's thought behind this.
3. Full credit to all the creative artists and authors in this world.

INTRODUCTION

I spent 17 years of my career working for someone else. Every month end, during those almost two decades, my ears yearned for the sweet SMS beep tun tun - "Update, your salary has been credited for this month."

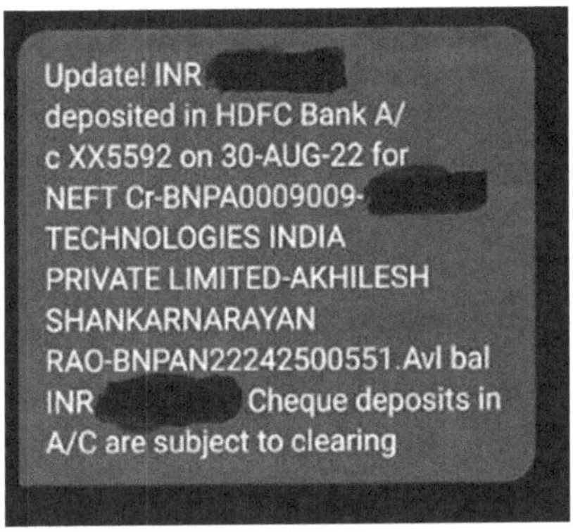

To receive this message, you have to work selflessly for the entire month. However, the point is you are working for someone else's goals.

"Love your job, but never fall in love with your company."

— Narayan Murthy

If you love your work and you are passionate about what you are doing, then you are blessed. Else, do not lie to yourself because every Monday morning when you wake up and if you aren't feeling good to go to work, you have the answer in your tone, "Oh, Sunday is over again." The routine of going to work and waiting for a salary is known to most working professionals, with a few exceptions!

Typical Mondays of an Employee

1. If you are dedicated to your project, you motivate yourself, because you have to motivate your teammates too.
2. You are going to meet important clients, which can be very significant as you are answerable. Also, your promotion is round the corner. In such scenarios, you know how to start your Mondays with full energy.
3. And you don't have a choice. Your boss told you to come early in the morning for a meeting.
4. There is a new colleague joining in. She is beautiful or he is smart. You want to be the first person to welcome! This may sound a little funny, but most of the time true!

You may see some parallels on the above lines when you typically start your working days.

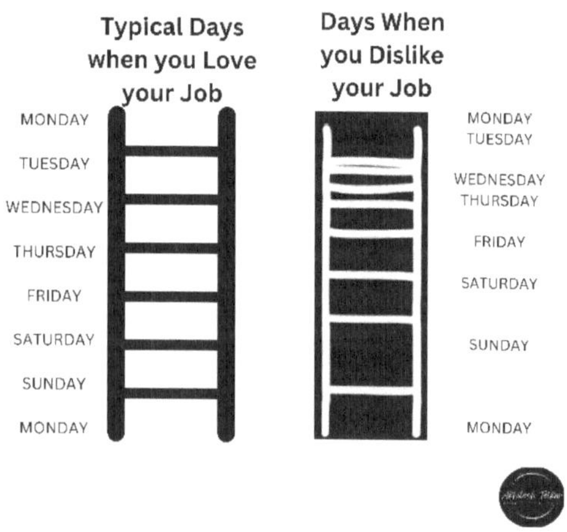

You could be concerned with running your family, taking more responsibilities, working hard, and doing whatever it takes.

Work-life is addictive, compulsive, never satisfied and out of balance. These seem to be too many adjectives but, unfortunately, they exist for most employees. Even though you want to come out of this situation, you can't. Unknowingly, you become a work alcoholic.

There could be undemanding expectations, unreal targets, and no holidays. You might be unavailable for your own self with your teeth sunk in never-ending tasks to complete.

You may have no time for family, functions, friends and get-togethers. There could be instances when you are not available when your loved ones need you the most.

I still remember my tour to Chandigarh for an important Installation — Asia's First Fully Automatic Fluoroscopy Machine getting installed in India. It was my privilege to represent the company because the machine was imported from Italy. Having been trained by Italian engineers, I was excited about meeting and learning from them. We had to maintain and train further hospital staff as well. For that Turnkey project, I spent almost three months in Chandigarh.

Mom called me and asked me to come home for Diwali. So, I sought permission from my company to return home - I got an odd response.

Besides offering me additional tips, my company suggested extending my deputation period. As I am a South Indian, home-side we eat a variety of foods every day. My mom's cooking was so delicious that I could not resist. However, being in North India, I had to feed on local meals like paratha and roti every day. It's impossible for a South Indian to withstand for long in the north in the absence of domestic food.

The climate was another challenging aspect for me. Bengaluru has pleasant weather all year round. However, in the Northern part of India, it's extremely cold and extremely hot in the seasons. And to add insult to injury, imagine when your boss says no to coming home on Diwali (Indian Festival). How would you feel especially when you are sick of food, weather and suffering from cold and food allergies?

You can't leave a job like this and you can't take it anymore.

Once you become a 'job seeker', you have to deal with it.

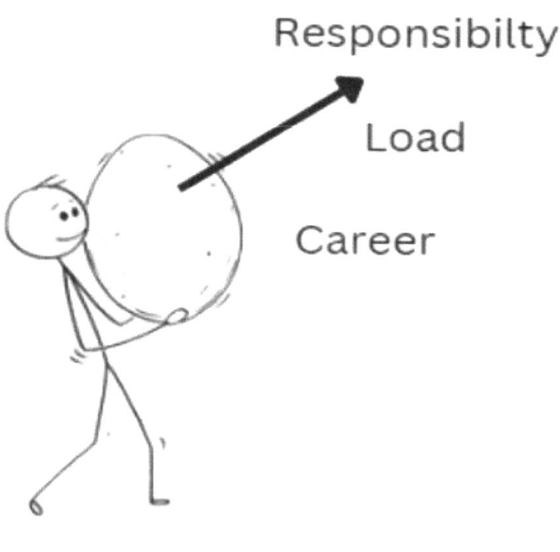

My biggest concern in my career was the fear of losing my job. What if my income ceases? How will I take care of my family? My future will be like a dark tunnel.

Although I was earning, I was not happy with the pace at which things were happening in my job life. Year by year, there was only a few percent of hike. I felt that in spite of all the sacrifices I made, the value I was getting in return was not proportionate.

That discontentment led me to the discovery of myself and the "Find U in "YOU" formula. This added wings to my life. So, in the book, I share with you the tools I have unearthed along the way to make my obsession work for me. Regardless of who you are, where you come from, what your family is like, or what your big dream is, if you are serious about your career growth and want to become unstoppable, this book will unlock your potential. It can help you to know your passion, guide your career in the right direction and make lots of money.

Before writing this book, I also authored the book "Find "U" in "YOU", which is my self-discovery.

"Unlock your potential and reap the success"

Find "U" in "YOU" helped me to have a framework, vision, mission and goals to achieve any objective.

When you start finding yourself and See "U" in "YOU" (Passion, Career & Paisa) as one connect, no one can stop you from becoming successful.

With your one hand on your heart and the other on your mind, say:

"I am ready for the change"

"I am ready to find Passion, Career & Paisa"

"I am ready to see myself as I am"

You can be successful without knowing yourself, but you can't reach the levels of success I am talking about without self-discovery. It's the single common factor that makes people super successful around the world. To show you how to know yourself and harness that "YOU" factor to build your success, I have broken this message into easy chapters.

Passion, Career & Paisa are the three domains of everyone's life - Now tell me who doesn't want to live a successful life? But what does it mean to be successful? In the following chapters, we learn more about the answers. However, before we proceed, here's a request: read this book as if your career is dependent on it.

The flow of this book is Self-Discovery, Personal story, Find "U" in "YOU", Career Journey, Character Building, Framework, Vision, Massive actions, Mindset, See "U" in "YOU", the ultimate winning formula.

Do we get the right education in our schools/colleges? Or are we prepared for machine language? Or we are conditioned for a certain type of Mindset?

Teachers- Study hard to be successful

Parents- Study and work hard to make money (Acchi padhiye se aachi naukri milti hai, aachi naukri se aachi kamai hoti hai aur aachi kamai se hi bade bante hain)

Relatives- What do you do in your life? (Beta kya karte ho? Kuch agay ka socha hai?)

This is quite normal that everyone gets to hear during the education or career start.

Let's understand what our inner voice says and how we get influenced by the outer voice (rather a noise).

Inner voice: It's "U" who makes you what you want to become.

Outer voice: It's circumstances that make you.

"A career is not about creating just a CV (Curriculum Vitae), A Career is not also about applying for a job and starting to work. Now, in this digital world, it's all about creating your 'value' and 'place' in the present market."

— Akhilesh Telkar

CHAPTER 1

CAREER

1.1 PENCIL TO PEN JOURNEY

We always wanted to do something else during our childhood days, but we could not convince our parents and teachers.

Irrespective of the outcome - we always wanted to play, engage in fun activities, not care about the rest of the world, not want to go to school and be busy in our own world.

We were taught in school to use pencils because if we made any mistake, we could Erase it.

As we grew up, we are allowed to switch from Pencil to Pen, because by that time we were supposed to nil/reduce our mistakes. This means as we mature, we should have a good understanding of worldly affairs, awareness of things and less room for mistakes.

As kids, we listened to our loved ones like parents, teachers, caretakers, seniors and elders. Obviously, they wanted our betterment, but they nurtured us with their perspectives and conditioning.

Now tell me – before coming to this world, did you have the option to choose your own parents?

No, right?

Did you choose your color, face, body shape, place of birth, living place, or personality?

Obviously, no.

How about your NAME?

No.

Your School?

Maybe, no,

Your school dress?

No.

You only had the meager option of choosing your daily needs. Rest all other things were beyond your control.

Your parents or caretakers were taking care of your needs and guiding you.

How about during college or a degree?

Some kids have the freedom to choose.

But still, because the fee was borne by parents - you had to compromise here as well.

Until college is fine.

How about going to a course or a job?

In some cases, parents raise their hands, saying, "We have already fed you for years. Now it's your time to go out and earn."

Some kids have the privilege to select further courses or certifications.

This is a crucial stage. I do not mean that you did wrong by listening to your caretakers. Of course, we must obey our elders. But at this juncture, if you do not take the reins of your life into your hands, you might find yourself in troubled waters. Whatever you choose now becomes your most important factor Brand **"CAREER"**.

Warning: So be wise to select the right pathway for you. Don't come under the influence of wrong advice- see who is guiding you- check if that person is successful or living a mediocre life.

Duniya ka Sabse Bada Rog, Kya Khayenge Log!
Check kar lena apna LOG, Nahi tho Career Ban na jaye Bhog!
(The Biggest Disease in This World Is, What Will People Say!
Check your people, otherwise, you may ruin your career while listening to others.)

So, do not be a part of the herd mentality or bother about what will others say if you do what you like. You will be happier.

So, what happened in our childhood?

If you notice, our mindset was not in control when we were children. We were blindfolded by the education system and got into the rat race, surrounding ourselves with limiting mindsets.

The ability to take risks and follow our dreams was never taught to us. To achieve your dreams, you need to chase them. Maintain faith in others while fulfilling your desires.

Do you wish to live an average life and allow your mindset to take control of your life? Or would you rather make changes to your life today, make your mindset stronger to fight against the average mindset, and have a better ending?

Some people recognize the need to switch to a growth mindset early and go on to live the life of their dreams. Some may be lucky because they got an environment where their parents, friends, or colleagues encouraged them from the beginning, and they became successful on their path.

For instance, in metropolitan cities, people are more business-minded and are willing to take risks. In Western countries, kids are encouraged to build their life around their passion, like Arts & Crafts, Entertainment, Sports and others.

But let us admit, not everyone is lucky enough to get that kind of environment. We rely on life-changing moments or incidents that help us realize the problem and focus on where we want to go.

I encountered a series of such incidents that helped me break free of the average mindset, and since then I have become unstoppable. Now I do not let a weak mindset overpower me.

I still bump into moments when my elders tell me to relax and take it easy. I listen to them sometimes as life is for living and not just grinding. But for the majority of the time, my strong mindset takes charge.

In fact, I enjoy it more when my strong mindset is in charge as I do not take my work as work.

In the game of cricket, if you see, some players perform better when batting first (check their records, they are more successful) and some players perform very well under pressure. They always like to win matches under pressure like Mahendra Singh Dhoni, Yuvraj Singh, Suresh Raina, Ravindra Jadeja, Anil Kumble - they are match winners. I too cherish being under pressure and performing during tough times.

This book is going to equip you with the exact formula that helped me. By applying this formula, you can become unstoppable and super successful!

See "U" in "YOU" is not one of those typical theoretical motivational books that pumps you up momentarily. This is a proven, practical step-by step-guide with easy implementation methods to transform your life!

By picking this book, you have proved that you are different, and you have recognized the strong mindset in you.

Now, here is an important question.

Are you ready to explore the secrets of a strong mindset and success and learn the formula?

Before writing this book, I browsed through many books, articles and videos. So, I have shared my learnings in this book. To achieve more clarity, 10 days at Vipassana helped me the most. I started to see the world in a new dimension and the new me within a few days of that discovery. I started working on important areas of life: Health, Wealth, Relationship and Career.

"The Most extraordinary people in World do not have careers. What they have is a CALLING." What a powerful quote by Vishen Lakhani!

This inspired me to learn Silva Technique by Mindvalley - will share more on this in a later part of this book.

After studying books of millionaires and billionaires around the world, I was forced to think about what makes them who they are. I spent thousands of hours understanding the secrets of the most super-successful people. I started to look for any blueprint, any mantra, or any formula that could be applied by anyone in his/her life to become super successful. Finally, I understood the ultimate formula to become unstoppable by picking up the common factors in them.

From Pencil to Pen journey came to light, as my goal of this book will influence you and millions of others around the world to create a new avatar by SEE "U" in "YOU".

Imagine a world full of love and care, where there is no value for this piece of paper (money), everything is available in abundance, anyone can use anything and live a life full of joy and happiness.

Sapna ek sundar duniya ka, jahan pe sirf pyar hi pyar ho... (A dream of a world where only love exists…)

Sapna ek sundar duniya ka, jahan kahin pe bi jayen, har jagha sirf khubsurat log hi mele... (A dream of a world where wherever you go, you only find people with much love...)

Sapna ek sundar duniya ka, jahan pe paise ki jarurat na ho, jo maange dilse, vo mele kushi se... (A dream of a world where money is not required to buy happiness...)

Sapna ek sundar duniya ka, jahaan koi ameer insaan na ho, koi garib na ho; har koyi samaan rahe... (A dream of a world where all are alike, no difference between rich and poor...)

Sapna ek sundar duniya ka, jahaan pe sabhi apne rahe, na ego, na dokha, na farebi... (A dream of a world where there is no place for ego, fear, or unfaithful...)

Sapna ek sundar duniya ka, jahaan rishton ka naam na ho, har koi hamara saathi ho... (A dream of a world with there is no caste or religion, where everyone is the same and everyone is ours...)

Sapna ek sundar duniya ka jahaan pe sirf pyar hi pyar ho, pyar hi pyar ho... (A dream of a world with much Love...)

"A dream is not what you see in sleep,
a dream is something that does not let you sleep."
— Dr. Abdul Kalam

Imagine if every person on this earth starts thinking with a positive frame of mind, fully and completely into their self-less broad mindset without any reservation, regret, or apology. Overnight, the world would be a different and better place. With everyone so focused on their productivity and creating their success, there would be no time for war, drugs, or other wasteful, unnecessary destruction. We have hit the levels of success previously by achieving what was thought impossible and inspiring one another to do more and be more.

The next chapters are built on this foundation, guiding you through the tough process of beginning to follow your Passion. It shines the torch on why it's important to "know your passion" before you made headway toward the world of careers.

In Chapter 1 – The Career: This chapter spotlights the ways you can learn for your career to dominate— your past, your thinking, your area of expertise, and your brand.

In Chapter 2 – The Passion: we will explore why you need to "starve the doubt," block out old beliefs and embrace haters. Passion is to build on that foundation, guiding you through the tough process of beginning to follow your Passion. You will learn why it's important to "know your passion" before you made headway to the world of careers.

Chapter 3 – The Paisa: explains why playing it safe is the most dangerous thing you can do— and how to stay mindful against great odds. These principles will guide you in your quest for success.

We have all read school textbooks that tell us to follow our academics. But while those books might offer an education path, how to implement that knowledge practically in our life remains unexplained.

This book will be honest and self-expressed. It will tear down the average mindset that has been spun so tightly around you by society. See "U" in "YOU" will help you unleash the power of obsession and then teach you how to take care of your PCP (Passion, Career & Paisa) to achieve your dreams.

ACTIVITY 1

Take a minute off:

Place one hand on your heart and the other on your mind and say-

"I am ready to Dream Big"

"I am ready to succeed in "Passion, Career & Paisa"

"I am ready to see this beautiful world"

1. Write a few lines about how has been your pencil-to-pen (childhood to now) journey (personal story)!

   ____

   ____

2. Write a few lines about what your biggest dreams have been so far.

   ____

   ____

Your level of success will be determined by your level of Character

If you are ready to take responsibility for your life and your career, and are ready to change your future and the world, then turn the page.

1.1.1 SELF-CHECK!

बनावट (Materialistic World)

सजावट (Make-up)

और दिखावट..(Show-off)

इन्ही के कारण आई है (because these reasons)

लोगों में गिरावट...! (the thinking of the people has deteriorated)

CHECK THIS OUT!

Who are the 5 people with whom you associate the most? These maybe close relatives, friends or neighbors.

Check how successful they are and see what type of career path they are in now and what they are doing.

Are most of them on the same ground or there are slight differences?

Examples:

1. Average Graduation
2. Average Grades
3. Average lifestyle

Motivational speaker Jim Rohn famously said that **we are the average of the five people we spend the most time with.** Look around if the people and friends on your list are screaming success, or if they are validating average.

Most people accept the idea of average because their parents and peers told them to settle for less rather than chase their dreams.

Now you have become a victim unknowingly. You try to become the same as they are by doing or thinking of doing the same type of studies, certifications, business, etc.

I know it must be hard to believe this.

Let me take a few names: Tony Robbins, Oprah Winfrey, Dan Lok, Grant Cardone, Vishen Lakhani, Sandeep Maheswari, Dev Ghadhvi. Most successful personalities came from poor backgrounds but still, they reached the success height which most people cannot.

Such influential people are surrounded by motivating and successful people. They live in a community where everyone is like-minded and their level of thinking is different from the mediocre mindsets, their frequency is different. Their programs or guidance are beyond our thinking. You never thought about it, or no schools have imparted such an education.

This is the thinking I want you to change when you hold this book. You must see the world from a different angle, change the average mindset, and become unstoppable.

You are the Way You Think

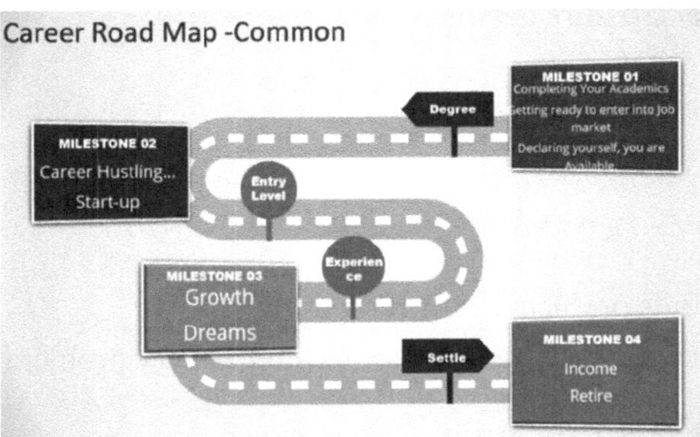

Fig.1 : Career Map

Common Career path mistakes in selections:

1. You start your career without knowing about your interest/passion.
2. You have the desire to do what you like to do, but you again come in the circumference of your home environment.
3. You never open up about discussing this further with your loved ones - hesitant to speak.
4. You fear attempting because the fear of failure bothers you the most.
5. You expect others to choose the right path in your career.
6. You select or keep in mind what your loved ones want.

Most career starters select a common path like the above.

Now the question that surfaces is: How to find the right career path for you? Well, you will find the right career path in the upcoming chapters.

As your mind begins collecting the conditioned data, an internal crossfire begins.

There are two voices in us:

1. AV= Angel Voice
2. DV= Devil Voice

DV- Finds problems with everything
AV- Knows and finds how to overcome every problem

D- Cry, creep, complain
A- Try to take conscious decisions

D- Thinks he knows everything
A- A good listener, open to learning

D- Postpone actions, wait for the perfect time
A- Takes actions, adapts to time

D- Afraid of losing
A- Never fear, think positive

D- Asks for people's opinion
A- Takes own decisions

D- Phobia of mistakes
A- Understands the importance of mistakes and is never fearful

D- Will have a lot of excuses
A- Always takes massive actions

D- Uncomfortable with change
A- Clarity on the process

D- Doesn't ask questions
A- Challenges oneself

D- Believes in trials and errors
A- Clarity in change and win, takes people along

D- Hesitates to invest in new ventures/platforms
A- Invests wisely, gives importance to self-development

D- No vision
A- Clear image of the future

D- Fears to take decisions
A- Focuses on actions

D- Stagnant in growth

A- Feeds every day, gets stronger

D- Complaints about the situation, people

A- Grateful, enjoys an abundance

Which voice do you allow to win; Angel or Devil?

Ans: ____________________

Your inner voice tells you to go beyond your limits, try new things, choose what you want and weed the success that you are dreaming of for long years. It always gives us hints about what we like most, but these might go unheard.

This bleak voice makes an appearance at times when opportunities knock on the door, comes in our dreams and sends signals but we tend to "Ignore".

We may want to do something but end up doing something else.

Our loved ones tell us to relax, go a little easy, start something not much risky, not work too much, life is for one time, enjoy this movement and that money is not everything. And you might be following the same like; getting a monthly salary to manage the expenses, taking credit to pay the bills and enjoying your weekends. Investigation into self-education could be the last option.

Some are lucky to get freedom with this approach, but they, one or the other way, find themselves under societal pressure.

They are in the race to build their "STATUS".

So, you could be under pressure of maintaining your social status so that you have your status in the society.

You may not want to disappoint your loved ones. Therefore, you do not want to take too many risks and hence, choose a safe mode.

However, the bitter truth is that you are working for someone else's goals. This may keep you at distant quarters from authority and enjoyment. You could be satisfied with what you have now. This may prevent you from thinking out of the box and planning your future. Even if you do chalk out a plan, you may not be able to stick to it.

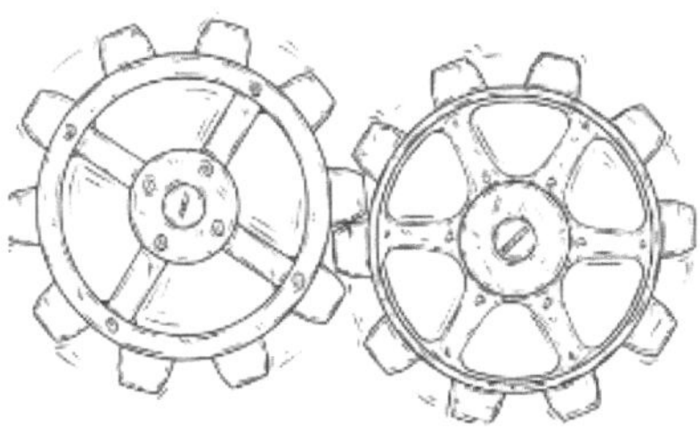

One thing you may face, which is very common, is that if you become obsessed with following the same regime, you may invite problems. Working on a never-ending task set by your boss may leave you with little time for your family.

You may face difficulties managing between work, career, and business.

Every successful person has to go through this, but the winner is the one who balances it all by following his/her passion, building the brand career and making lots of paisa.

Warning: You cannot get far on the road to success if you do not invite this problem. Don't be surprised if it's challenging, that it's risky, and if it will lead you to a place you have never been before.

If you are not mentally prepared, it is not for you. You may face more difficulties than you expect.

This book solves such areas of life in a simplified manner. You may have to identify your inner strength, bring more clarity and prepare for the best.

I will walk you through some key exercises you can practice finding out what you want most in life.

People often ask me, "What does it take to be more successful?"

Understanding life and balancing important factors are essential to be successful.

Achieving "Health, Wealth, Relationship and Career" is the key to success.

So, start empowering your powerful Vision, Big Mission and living with your Goals.

Here are 4 important factors to consider:

1. Passion that pays
2. Self-determination with micro-niche

3. Willingness to learn quickly and adapt to the situation
4. The ability to use your God-given assets productively

Then they ask, "How to do this? What's the path?"

Find "U" in "YOU" is the first step.

(E-book on Amazon Kindle - https://www.amazon.in/dp/B0B5HN2TLS)

Whether you are a fresher, just starting a career, experienced, business owner, trailblazer, freethinker, artist, athlete, inventor, salesperson, creative, or engineer, I know you are someone who strives for success and refuses to settle for less.

This book encourages the desire to do more, build a never-give-up attitude and develop the hunger to do more hard work. It helps you harbor an achiever mindset and outshine the achiever hidden inside you.

I will help you establish your brand career and show you how to grow to heights despite all obstacles and competition.

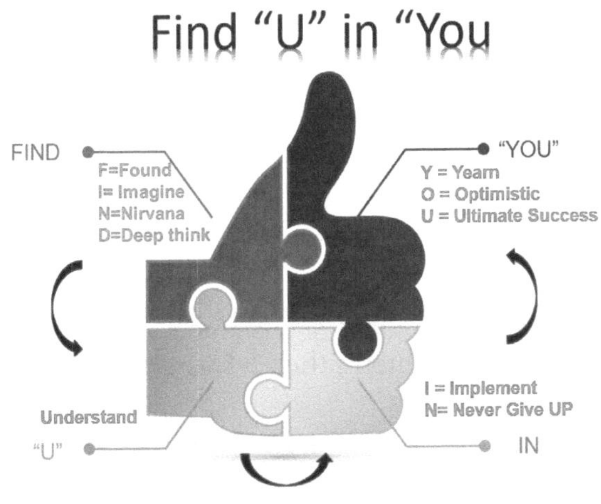

Framework: fig 2

The first step to success is self-discovery. A person who knows very early about his passion, purpose and desires stands out in the competition. You enjoy true freedom and total control of your life—personally, emotionally and financially.

Therefore, you must know what your passion is, regardless of your studies or academics. What if you completed your degree in computer science and you were applying for a software development job? Do you enjoy coding or developing?

For instance, if you are passionate about your singing skills, you know how songs are developed and can sing along as an engineer. If you are a good software developer and you love singing, imagine you are applying for a job with a company or media that specializes in singing or entertainment. You can combine your class passion and technology to make passion tech so simple.

You will be at your very best: hyper-focused, persistent beyond understanding and creative to the point of appearing magical. Such a state means that you are operating at the levels you were always meant. You can pull others up to their full potential and possibilities.

Trust my words, just first commit to changing your life and this book will amplify all your positive thoughts.

If we have an agreement, then let us get ready to See "U" in "YOU".

Please read out the below mutual See "U" in "YOU" agreement loud before you sign it:

ACTIVITY 2 : SELF-AGREEMENT

Keep one hand on your heart and the other on your mind, and say:

"I am ready to find myself"

"I am ready to succeed in "Passion, Career & Paisa"

"I am ready to see my best version"

I, (Your Name)______________________________ pledge my career to become treated as a lifeline. From today, I take full control of my health, wealth, and relationships.

I would never ever think of anything that is average.

I will dream big and will put in 10 times more effort to make things happen. I vow to cut all the loser friends, garbage habits, and negative thoughts out of my life. I am born with a genius inside me, that I will bring to this world and build a brand-new career by following what I love.

I believe in Myself

I believe in my Power

I believe in my Future

I believe I can unleash my potential, re-discover my present and re-ramp my future

I will create my own story

Yes, I love myself, I am the hero of my life.

I will build my legacy starting today, one step at a time. I will have the best of family life, health, and financial life. I will work hard, smart, and train every single day. I will never ever give any excuses and will take full ownership of all the events happening in my life.

I will make my family proud of me. I pledge to become non-stop, a massive action-taker.

Sign ....

Date..................

1.2 : INITIALS OF CAREER

I wanted to connect with the readers in the deepest format ever I can. Therefore, I have shared my life experiences, including curiosity, intensity, love, and secrets to unlock your potential.

Hum honge kamyab,
(We will succeed)

Ek din, mann mein hai vishwas,
(One day, we will, I have faith)

Pura hai vishwas
(I completely believe we will)

Hum honge kamyab.
(We will succeed)

— ***Girija Kumar Mathur***

Whether you start your own business or choose the right company to work for, cultivate your passion for yourself or the company. Think and act as if you are in charge of everything that happens.

1. Know the business
2. Do more with less
3. Go beyond your job description

If you don't know how to sell yourself better than others, then you cannot position yourself in this market.

If you cannot position yourself, then you cannot grab the opportunity.

Then how will you succeed in your career?

Be mindful that we were all born to be great, but most of us decide to go against nature and never realize our purpose. It is time to start thinking and discovering your true purpose.

I grew up in an environment with average schooling, an average company and an average middle-class life (not blaming anyone or the situation). Everyone was happy and satisfied with the average-paying jobs, the average grades, and the average lifestyle. Not that anyone was bad, but the truth is - they limited themselves to an average life. And even I made the same mistake which cost me so many years. In 2022, I was awakened to this factuality and started investing in myself.

The journey of pursuing my passion started, which imparted a new meaning to my life.

Earlier, I was unaware of my potential. I seldom tried to know about my purpose. Therefore, I was living a meaningless life, and ruining my career in the hands of others.

I didn't have any paternal legacy that could lead me to the land of the rich, lend me lakhs of rupees for my first business, assist with new connections to start a new business, or help me with ideas to succeed in a business.

16-20 - Danger

20-30 - Soldier

30-40 - Hunter

40-50 - Beggar

50-60 - Wheel puncher

(Description of lifecycle by Upendra)

My Story in Short

8-16 – Khel kum kar, padai kar (play less and study more)

16-20 - Kam ke saath padai kar (study while you work)

20-30- Struggler

30-37 - Hunter continues...

— Akhilesh Telkar

"The two most important days in your life are the day you're born and the day you discover why."

— Mark Twain

1.2.1 My Parents were two different personalities

My mother was a 10th pass who had very little familiarity with the outside world until her marriage. My dad was the first to go to college from his family and completed a degree during the 1970s. He was an ambitious young man with an entrepreneurial spirit who believed his dreams were within his reach. Dad ventured into a retail business, merchant business and then tried his hands at politics.

He was affluent at that time, owning good property and making money.

However, because of his political involvement, dad suffered a terrible loss. Several of his close ones cheated on him upfront. So, he decided to start a new life from scratch.

Using the money he had saved, he became a cloth merchant, embarking on yet another new career.

One day, he was returning home after wrapping up his business for the day. Amidst that dark night, it was pouring heavily as dad made his headway to home. He was holding a bag of money, which was our school fees. Suddenly, dad noticed someone following him, so he speeded his steps. He had brisked for a few yards when he got stabbed badly on his back. Dad fell in the middle of the road. When he regained consciousness, he noticed that his bag had been stolen. Somehow, dad managed to reach home, but that incident shook him to the core. The worry of how he would pay the school fees of his kids started to escalate. On the other hand, his new business had yet to take off, which was aborted due to that money loss. That unfateful episode broke him, and from there he almost felt like he had failed. On the night before the Makar Sankranti (a South Indian festival), he complained of pain in his chest, so my mom rushed him to the hospital.

I was 8 years old at that time. When I visited the hospital to see my dad, I noticed him lying on the bed with an oxygen mask tied to his mouth. The ECG machine was making tee-tee sounds. With dread in my eyes, I gazed at the medical equipment around him; the LEDs, the wires and the knobs. Then I saw my dad gesturing me from his eyes to come near him. He asked me to take money from his pocket. I placed my hands in his loose pocket and got 3 coins 20+20+10=50 paisa. That was the asset he had given me.

The new year has just begun. It was 1992. In South India, after the New Year, we celebrate Makar Sankranti on the

15th of January. On that day, I was thrilled because I used to go and meet all my friends dressed in new clothes and feast on sweets. In Kannada, we call ellu (sesame seeds), bella (jaggery), and kabbu (sugarcane).

Even small things were fascinating to me, like wearing a new dress, eating delicious sweets and seeing different colors of peppermint. The day was usually spent distributing sweets, ellu, bella, and sugarcane to the neighbors. As I ran around that day, I was so tired that I fell asleep as soon as I got into bed.

Around 2 am, my sister suddenly shook me and asked me to get up.

Akka: Hey, get up, get up!

Me: Nooo... (I was unable to open my eyes, so I turned a deaf ear to my sister's voice, pulled the bedsheet over my face, and slept again.)

But my sister continued to wake me up.

Akka: The car has come in front of the house. We have to hurry up and getup (my sister said in a louder pitch).

As I heard the word car, I got up in an instant and tried to open my little eyes. It was Vishnu uncle's blue Ambassador car in which we used to go for our family trips. Riding in the car itself was a tremendous feeling, and I was super excited.

My sister locked the house, rushed towards the car, and opened the backseat door.

It was a dark midnight; I didn't get much time to see what was happening. As I tried to get into the car, I saw my mom inside the car, crying. Then I noticed I didn't have the space to sit because my dad was sleeping on my mom's lap. There was the smell of flowers inside the car. When I understood the situation, mom uttered, "Everything is finished, nothing can be done. Your dad is no more."

The following day, at 8 am, I was playing with my favorite tennis ball outside my uncle's home, and people started coming to see my dad's face one last time. I was unaware of the situation and what was happening. I only knew, "My dad sleeps for long hours, and mom doesn't."

In the afternoon, my dad was taken for the final rituals. My uncle asked me to change into a dhoti (thin white shallya) and sit near a water tank. I was not sure what was happening. Suddenly, one barber came with a foldable knife. He directed me to sit straight and not to move. I asked, "Hey, what are doing? Don't do anything." I shouted, "Ma Ma see here, uncle wants to take my hair" Even after so many retaliations, the barber took out all strands and made me bald. Suddenly one bucket of cold water was poured on my head (I am not too fond of cold water). I screamed so loud that everyone looked at me. I was shivering, realizing something terrible was happening and unsuitable for my future.

The next day, I recall sitting on a cycle bar, paddled by my uncle. We were passing by our school field near my home, looking at the Field. I was thinking of playing cricket later in the evening with friends. On the other hand, my uncle had to say something which I had never thought of. He said that I had to take up the colossal responsibility of the family. His words were completely alien to me. Imagine an 8-year-old kid has to take responsibility for the family; how he might feel.

What do you think he can do? One more thing my uncle told me was, "The only way to get all your effort paid is by hard work."

My mother found herself a widow at thirty-seven with two girl children and one boy. My mom was in great trouble with no roof over our heads, no money and no income. she was just 10th pass and had no professional skills she could use to bring in new income. Mother had dedicated her life to being a wife and mother. And now she had to figure out how to conserve the money my dad had left and grow it to provide for the kids. It was a big challenge, as my mother had no college education and did not have earning potential. She was like a bundle of nerves.

To mother, the future expenses were a threat, so she quickly began to downsize. She immediately put my father's dream site on sale. We were forced to live in a rented house, a small house in a tiny lot, surrounded by block houses that looked alike. There was grief- we all missed our backbone. On top, the society's pressure and kids' demands, my mom was scared, and I could feel it. There was constant anxiety that was evident.

While other boys my age played sports, enjoyed summer holidays and summer camps, I was at home, worried about the cost of basic necessities and so on.

In India, arranging the marriage of a girl child without a dowry was very difficult, especially in the 1990s. And my mom had two girl children. I was oblivious to what was happening. I was in my own world, still playing, and asking a few questions that mom did not have answers to.

I would often find myself curious and agitated. And the more I had them, the more I knew I was both wrong and right. I knew I should be grateful—so many other people had less than us. But I was also aware there was truth in what I was thinking. Why should anyone have only enough money to get by and still need to worry about money? When things would cool down, I would try to explain to my mother it wasn't that I didn't appreciate everything she did for us or that I wasn't grateful for everything we had. The reality was I would continue to have this push/pull, right/wrong argument about scarcity and money with myself and others for years to come.

I didn't know it then, but that time seeded something that would later drive me in life. As much as I loved, admired, and appreciated my mom for what she did to ensure we had clothes, food, and a roof over our heads, I didn't want to live my life in a constant state of worry. At the age of 16, I vowed to my mother, "When I grow up, I am going to get rich so we never have to worry about not having enough money, and when I do, I am going to help a lot of people."

My mother had that look on her face that every parent has. She was furious, disappointed, and frustrated. Still, I felt an overwhelming sense of powerlessness, knowing I couldn't do anything about anything at the time.

I tried being grateful for and appreciative of all that we had, but it never sat right with me. The whole thing seemed so screwed up. I was 8 years old, my dad was no more, all the property was gone, mom was living in fear, and I was supposed to be grateful? I wasn't grateful—I was out of temper!

I slowly realized that I have to start earning fast to free up my mom from her responsibilities. During the vacations of my 9th standard, when all my friends had planned their summer trips and played in their free time, I started going for part-time learning jobs without salary (electrician).

1.2.2 This middle-class thing sucks

"Zindagi kitni karwaten badalti hai
(Life takes so many twists and turns)
Kabi pareshani, kabi nadaani
(Sometimes troubles, sometimes innocence)
Ruk, abhi hai lambi khahaani...
(Stop! Still yet to see long life story...)

— Akhilesh Telkar

I am going to get mine!"

29th March was my birthday, the same day I completed my public 10th exams. All my friends had planned for higher studies in new colleges – but what about me? I was clueless. I also wished to attend college, but my uncle called me to help me learn the electrical work at his shop. He said if I knew the electrician's work, I could start my shop and lead the rest of my life peacefully. So I went to my mother's native place Haveri (in the district of Karnataka) for three months.

My 10th results got announced, and I passed in the first class. Holding my mark sheet, I started crying, thinking about what to do next. My hands were rough and rugged because of lifting heavy objects during three months of hardship work at an electrical shop. No play, no enjoyment, no excitement in that work- only work, work continued day and night.

After looking at my results, my mother and sisters decided to send me for further studies. I was not a failed student nor was I a lazy gully boy to be punished for not studying. Following my wish – I joined a Diploma in E & E.

I continued to study and did a part-time learning job for 3 years. Do you know how much my first salary was? Any guesses? It was a Sonata watch I got for working in a refrigerator shop during my study breaks when I was 16 years old.

Choosing the right degree and college is very crucial. The parents look for many options, they run around for advice, and they try to give their children the best education so that when the kids complete their degree, they land a good job and get settled.

Here are some major problems among most middle-class parents. They decide their children's careers based on the number of opportunities available in the market, the nearness of the school/college so that it is convenient to communicate and the fee structure, irrespective of children's interests or skills/passion.

Had I not enrolled for a diploma in E & E I had to take the biggest challenge, which was returning to hardship labor work.

1.2.3 Choosing shop work versus college was challenging

On the first day, I was thrilled to go to college. As my mom could not afford to send me to a private college because of high fees, so I joined a government college 17 km away.

I used to walk for 3 km from my house to the Shivamogga bus stop, then board a government bus to Bhadravathi bus stop and again march to college for around 2.2 km (my daily to and fro).

I continued to study and did a part-time learning job for 3 years.

I studied 12 subjects a year for 3 years. I was eager to fetch a job so that my earnings could start, which would relieve my mom of her responsibilities.

As I used to travel for 17 km every day, when exams were round the corner, I felt that I was not getting ample time to study because of traveling. So, I decided to rent a room for 2 months in Bhadravathi at a walkable distance from my college. My friends also suggested group studies.

As the room rent and food expenses had to be borne, I started eating limited food in a mess nearby. I studied harder, which helped me a lot. It was my first time away from home. I had to manage in the amount given by my mom. That was when I felt the pinch of living alone with a scanty budget.

There were campus interview calls in the final year.

A few companies came to take interviews. Before the interview, there was a written exam, which I could not qualify.

The second time, we were supposed to go and write in Hassan for BHEL apprenticeship - written exams.

It appeared that many questions I answered were not in the syllabus, either I didn't study my textbooks adequately or the exam questions were difficult.

Again, I failed to qualify. That day, I felt bad about the situation, because I was under pressure to grab the opportunities, as I was in a hurry to get into some job.

I became doubtful if I would be able to pursue higher studies. My mother could not afford to pay for an engineering degree.

Until the end of my exams, no one told me what to do, and neither college taught us which career to choose. Besides, my mother was unable to pay for further studies. It was a typical lower middle-class issue.

There are no other choices, we grow-up and take responsibility. This is how the careers of most lower middle-class kids get started!

I believe that I have the qualities of clay. Whichever mold you put me in, I take that shape. I can adapt quickly to any situation. I am a loyal follower, a good listener, believe in change and a creative thinker.

No matter how many times I tried to convince myself of my mother's logic, it never added up for me. The family was terrified every time we went to the grocery store because we were worried about running out of money.

I was unable to do anything to remedy the family's situation at that time. I was young and frustrated and, frankly; I didn't know how to take the bull by the horns. With too much time on my hands and no strong mentorship in my life, I was becoming silent and helpless.

I was also a big fan of sports and average in my studies; I was playful in school, college and would often go out to play. Besides, I hung around with friends. It was not that I was not interested in studies, but I was more magnetized to drawing, dancing and sports that came naturally to me. There were opportunities, but due to a lack of money and guidance, I could not avail those. I always wished someone from the sky would appear in front of me as a godfather, recognize my talent, encourage me to go to the next level, and support me to unlock my potential. (Aha Aha-just imagine)

All of us have potential and hidden talents, however, we need the right guidance and opportunity to showcase those.

Instead of saying "Beta Job Dundo" I wish someone would have told me "Beta Passion Dundo."

— Akhilesh Telkar

If all parents in the world understand this, the world will be more joyful.

ACTIVITY 3

Take a minute off:

Keep one hand on your heart and the other hand on your mind and say-

"I am ready to Dream Big"

"I am ready to succeed in "Passion, Career & Paisa"

"I am ready to take challenges"

1. How was your education started? Did the home environment play a major role in your career?

 ____

 ____

 ____

2. Write 3 challenges that you faced at the start of your career.

 ____

 ____

 ____

1.3 AFTER GROWING UP

As kids growing up, we are all very teachable. We go to school and become sponges, learning everything that is placed in front of us. And then the worst possible thing happens: We get a degree. To the world, that degree means you know something, but to most people, it means you are done learning.

Why do you like to relive your childhood days? If given the option to time-travel to the school days - would you opt in? Most likely, yes. We relish the phase when we were of our free will, not this materialistic life which we have now right.

After returning to my little house, I visited my astrologer uncle Sridhar Rao Telkar to seek his advice. He used to read the astroscope and tell people about the shubh time, good muhuraths (favorable times), guidance on what to do and when to start, He examined my astroscope and gave me a piece of paper uttering words like Gurubala, good timing, some pooja, this year, you do this and time will be favorable after so and so years, etc. He added, "Wherever you get a job, the company should be benefitted because of my work; more than you getting benefitted." Then told to meet him after one week and advised me to prepare my bio-data.

However, I did not think much about that and rather ruminated over my future. I stopped focusing on where I had been and started looking toward where I wanted to go. I knew I wanted to be very successful, to own a house, car, lots of money and become famous. But it seemed very far away from me at that movement.

I knew the first step to getting on the track to success was to help myself. I couldn't start helping others until I got my own life in order. I had to build my sense of self before I could get others to believe and trust me.

But where could I start? I had no friends, no support, no influences, no background, and no one to guide me.

I got my first job in Shivamogga as a sales executive.

My salary was fixed at Rs. 1500/month. That company had several branches all over Karnataka. The day I joined, I heard from my manager who was on a phone call with the other branch manager, that our branch sales were dropping.

After the call, my manager called me and said, "Look, we have to increase our sales this year, this is why you have been appointed for this job. You will be trained for one week at the front desk. Learn about the products, attend to the customers, start building a relationship with customers, then after one week, take the bike and go for sales."

His phone rang again, and he left the place. With a big open mouth, I was thinking, how can I do this? Imagine, for the first time after finishing my studies going to work, the most significant task in front of me, the enormous task, was not sales; it was driving a bike. I had a dream to sit on a two-wheeler the day I bought my own and not use others'. After hearing from my manager now, I had only one week to learn a two-wheeler, thinking and fearing how will I go to the field for sales. What if my manager came to know that I didn't know to drive a two-wheeler? It would become a big problem.

After attending the first day of training, I rushed to my cousin's house immediately and told him that there was a problem. I told him that I did not know how to drive a bike. And that my manager wanted me to do the sales from next week onwards on a two-wheeler, roam around the city and bring sales for the company. My brother understood my fear and said, “Relax, come to me at 7 am every day and I will teach you how to ride a bike (Baapre. I got much relieved after hearing those words from him).

The next day morning, my brother and I went to the field.

Bro: Turn on the Key, kick, first gear- release the clutch slowly.

I turned on the key, kicked holding the clutch, and released the clutch immediately.

Burrrr...Jump…Off… ”Omg, it's scary,” I said.

Bro: Do you want to kill me?

Wait, don’t release the clutch so immediately...

Me: Ok, one more time.

Bro: This time, first check if the bike is in neutral; after that kick, hold the clutch, put in the first gear, then slowly release the clutch while gradually accelerating.

Me: Neutral? How do I know the bike is in neutral?

Bro: See, there is a green light indicator, which lights up when the gear shaft is turned to neutral.

Me: Every expert was once a beginner, got it; let me try once more.

Bro: Yes.

Me: Key On, I turned the gear to neutral, kicked and then started accelerating, burr, burr... it sounds nice when we do this in the bike.

Bro: Change the gear to get in motion.

Me (pressing my left forefoot hard): It's not changing.

Bro: Hey, stop stop-stop, turn it off.

Me: Ok.

Bro: I forgot to tell you, there are different types of bikes. In some bikes, the gears shift with the forefoot and with the hindfoot in others. In this bike, you have to push with your hindfoot for all four gears.

Me: Alright, let's do it again.

I turned on the key, switched it to neutral, kicked, then left foot back press, holding the clutch tightly and slowly accelerating, burrrrrrr…

Bro (screaming): Hey, don't do that; reduce the accelerator and slowly release the clutch, then give a little accelerator.

This time, I did it correctly. The bike moved, and the smile on my face grew big as I successfully got it in motion.

The practice went on for three more days; then, in the office, the office boy was on leave; the manager told me to go to the bank and gave me the two-wheeler key.

Test Time: I took the key as if I had been driving a bike for a long time.

Sat on the bike, again the same steps – turn on, neutral, kick, hold the clutch and press back. My manager was watching me from the window. I was thinking about why the bike was not moving; I tried again by accelerating.

Still, the bike did not move an inch. I pressed hard at the back shaft of the gear.

My manager said loudly, "Hey, change gears to the front."

Omg- I forgot that it was a different two-wheeler; I got down from the bike as if I knew everything. Intentionally, I moved away from my manager's sight so that he did not feel I was a new learner and didn't know how to drive a bike.

Somehow, I was able to move the two-wheeler that day and felt relieved.

Find "U" in "You": "Fear of unknown to knowing a new skill."

Next time, I was more confident in driving any bike. I was thrilled when I saw a new bike. I felt crazy while driving as if I had got new wings.

"The expert in anything was once a beginner."

— Helen Hayes

On the other side, I did not know about repair or electrical work – it never interested me. I had learned those things as a part of my work, as I did not have any other option.

I went to the field for sales. The products I sold were - panel boards, motors, switches, gears and electrical cables.

These are not interesting products for house construction people in the city and are mainly for village people or farmers who need them for their sites.

One day, my manager was not happy with the branch sales. So, he sent me to the field to bring some new orders.

As I was not aware of the market to target, I visited under-construction sites, thinking they might require motors and switches for their houses. On one such day, I visited a rich Arecanut market (mandi) person's house. The security guard gave me the owner's number. So, I called him to pitch my products. Interestingly, he told me that he was looking for wirings for his under-construction house and asked me to visit Arecanut mandi. So, I went to him the next morning.

I did not have a phone, any communication was done through the landline of the office.

Upon meeting that man, I noted his requirements on a piece of paper. Then I returned to the office to show the list to my manager and get the rates. My manager was quite happy. The next morning, I again drove to the house owner and gave him the rates. To my surprise, after a negotiation call with my manager, the owner agreed to give the cheque for Rs, 47000.

I got my first sales ORDER.

My sales CAREER started....

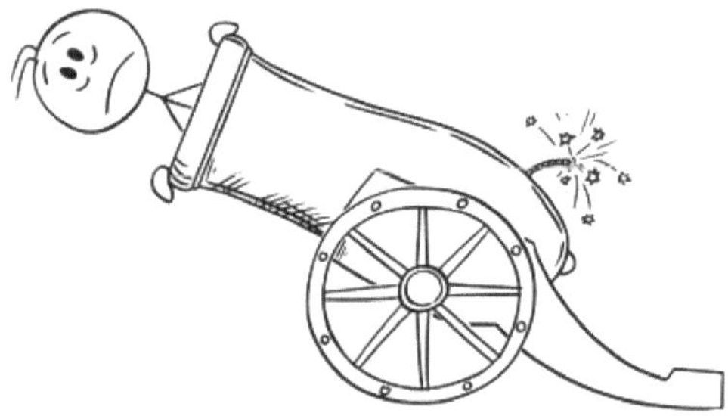

I had never done sales before. I was hungry to get into some job, so I just took to sales as it came. However, the results were quite good for the branch. But I worked in that company for only 3 months because I wanted to do more. My uncle had told me that if I wanted to grow fast, the only way was to get bigger opportunities, which were available only in metropolitan cities.

My manager called us for a monthly sales meeting.

Manager: This month, I am happy to present the sales of my branch.

Accountant: Yes, sir, we have good sales compared to the last few months.

Manager: I would like to continue with this team and grow like this.

Accountant: Sir, Akhilesh wants to leave this job and go to Bangalore, it seems.

Manager: What! Really, why so?

Accountant: Not sure what he sees in metro cities that he can't do here.

After settling at that company, I got a total of Rs. 4500 for 3 months. I said to my mom that the amount was enough to go to Bangalore and start work there because there were limited growth opportunities in the small town.

I had seen the accountant working at the same level for the last 10 years, and his salary was still low. He was not growing as he should have. I consider myself a growth-oriented person, and I can't stay in one place.

It was a scary decision; going to Bangalore without a job was difficult.

Following my uncle's words that if you want more enormous opportunities, you need to work in bigger cities; I took the bold decision.

So I boarded a bus with the quest to make big in life: 'Namma Bengaluru, I am coming', ready to bend-a-kal-uru (Bendakaluru).

1.3.1 Initial struggle days

I committed to everything that came my way. I aspired for a decent job and a monthly salary. I was not much privileged as I did not have any additional degree. Another certification would have incurred money, and I had no godfather who could directly land me a dream job.

In Jan 2005, before leaving Shivamogga, I called one of my uncles, Manjunath Rao Gujjar, a retired government medical officer in Bangalore.

I carried Rs. 4500 in my pocket and never looked back. My uncle was the biggest supporter when I started my career; I informed him about coming to Bangalore and requested for shelter. I said that I was searching for a job, and would vacate as soon as I got one.

His famous dialogue was, "If you want to achieve something big in life, you must dream big and a city like Bangalore is the best option. You have to drink the water of Bangalore thoroughly," which means once you dive into the water, you will learn to swim anyhow.

> *"To learn swimming you need to get into the water first. Naturally, the situations will teach you how to swim."*
>
> *— Akhilesh Telkar*

The initial days were easy-going; I learned about Bangalore city, places, and commutation, and met a few friends already in Bangalore. Everyone advised me to come with my resume.

Up to that date, I wasn't prepared with any resume. I had no mobile as there was a charge of Rs. 3/- minute even for incoming calls. The cyber centers used to charge Rs. 20/- hour for the internet usage. The only way to call home and friends was a Re. 1 coin yellow box called Coin Box from the STD booth.

BMTC's (Bangalore Metropolitan Transport Corporation) bus pass was for Rs. 300/month and Rs. 20/- day in 2005.

Four months went by; the money was leaking out, but the job was not yet confirmed; I tried all my contacts, but to no avail. Everyone who said, "Come to Bangalore, you will have a bright future," had disappeared. I started feeling lonely on the streets. My CV printout was costing more than my snacks, and I could not understand what to do. My uncle told me to register with the Employment Bureau at Chamarajpet, Bangalore, and tried a few non-relevant interviews, which didn't work for me.

Getting a job became a challenge with every passing day, and I had a taste of failure before even starting. My pockets were getting empty; I had to think twice before eating anything. I started calculating the expense for 30 days of survival, Rs. 10/ meal each day equaled 10x30 = Rs. 300, but I needed money for the monthly pass to commute.

Rs. 4500/- suddenly felt like significantly less; many thoughts played in my mind. Should I go back to Shivamogga for an Rs. 1500/- month job, or will I have to learn electrical repair work again? I started thinking of options. That was something I had not expected. I wanted to achieve something bigger in life, but now I was feeling shallow and started losing hope.

I was not applying for jobs in the right way. I was at the wrong places, visiting the wrong people.

I had prepared a CV by spending Rs. 20/- hour in a cyber center with an old version system. Without taking help or support from any career advice, I was thinking of visiting companies, going to security and giving my crap CV to get my first job.

Instead of focusing on beautifying my CV which would represent my personality and create an opportunity for me,

I was doing all the wrong things. That landed me in great trouble and ended up being jobless for almost 4 months.

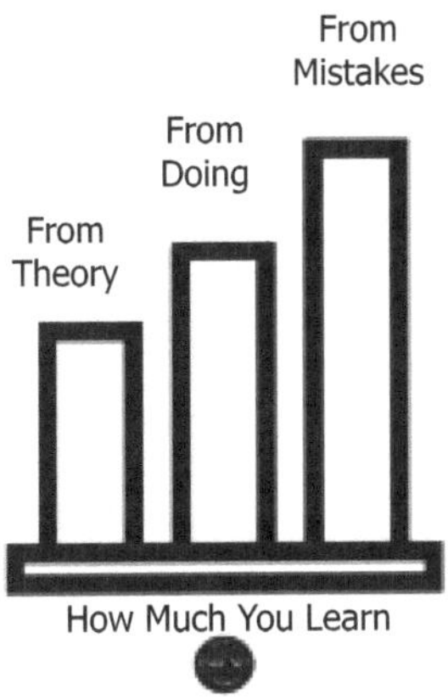

1.3.2 Customer care first job

As usual, after trying for the whole day, I was having Rs. 10 meal at a restaurant when I saw my senior passing by.

Senior: You were my junior in college!

Me: Yes, thanks for recognizing me.

Senior: What are doing here?

Me (saying to myself: Having my Rs. 10 meals): Ahh, looking for a job.

Senior: Oh, ok (as if he will get me a job now).

I asked him for the contact number of didi (Nirmala didi whom I used to admire a lot during my college days).

Senior: I don't know her personal number, you can note down her home number.

Me: Great, thank you - noted the number.

Senior: Ok see you, getting late.

Me: Thank you very much.

I rushed to the telephone booth and called that number. It rang, but nobody picked the call.

I dialed again - the number you have called is busy.

After a few minutes, I tried again.

An uncle answered the call this time: Yaru (who is this)?

Me: Nanu uncle, Nirmala didi na mathad bekittu (Wanted to speak to didi).

Uncle: Neen yarappa (Who are you)?

Me: We studied in the same college, my name is Akhilesh.

Uncle: She works in Bangalore, call on her mobile.

Me – Uncle, please give her mobile number.

Uncle - Ok, note down.

I was so happy to finally get her number.

But I did not call her that evening, as I was penniless. So, I backtracked and requested my uncle to allow me to make a call.

He gave his mobile (Rs. 6/call - so imagine and compare today)

I dialed didi's number.

Me: Hi didi.

Didi: Hey, hi Akhilesh.

Me: Yes, thank you for recognizing me.

Didi: Of course, why not, how did you get my number?

I explained to her how I got it.

Didi: So what are you doing?

Me: In Bangalore now, looking for a job.

Didi: Come tomorrow at 9 am to Rajajinagar, HP petrol bunk.

Me (with a happy note): Thank you and see you tomorrow.

I did not call her for a job, I just wanted to speak to her before leaving. But see how the universe plays a role.

I met her and she introduced me to the owner of her company. And guess what, – my job got confirmed.

Someone has rightly said, **"Everything happens at the right time, at the right place."**

Through my goodwill during my college days, I got my first job in Bengaluru after struggling for almost 4.5 months.

I was appointed as a Customer Service Representative at LG CDMA mobile center for Rs. 2500/month in the year 2005.

It was just peanuts to start with, but at least it was feeding my stomach and allowing me to stay in Bangalore, and pay for the food, roof overhead, and travel expenses.

It was a front desk job in a mobile service center. The clients were the ones looking for a mobile repair or buying some accessories. Whenever any customer came at the front desk, the first task was to enter the details in the job card and take customer complaints. So, on my first day, it was very new to me. Didi told me to just observe how she made the entry. She explained to me how customer entries were to be made, how to use the system, etc. and in case of any doubt, she asked me to call her. That was how my first day started. I was very happy that I got a very nice place to sit.

It was an AC room, and I had a system to operate. I had got the opportunity to work, so I was quite excited. However, the first difficulty I encountered was the language. For any customer who walked in with a mobile complaint, I was supposed to speak in English. Until that time, I had never spoken in English with anyone. So, communication was a challenge and my first week was horrible. I used to gesture to them in yes or no.

I was not in a position to speak to them fluently and confidently. One thing I understood was that to survive in Bangalore, English is a must. I realized that if I did not learn English, the chances of losing good opportunities were high. So, I set my mind to improving my English. I developed a habit of reading English newspaper. As days went by, I started learning a few words to a few sentences. My language was not that good but okay to attend to some customers. Comparatively, the task of call entry was easy as I had to enter some 60 to 80 entries without difficulty. This continued for 3 months. It was just an inter-period, so the job was getting easier day by day. Then one fine day, my manager called me and said, "Your entries are going very nicely and I see very few mistakes compared to the first month." I still remember when I got my first salary of Rs. 2500 and I went to withdraw it so that I could send that amount home. I was quite happy because I used to get the monthly salary without any problem. But after 5 months, I started feeling that was not what I was supposed to do. The customer care job was only about the job card entry and attending to customer complaints. It was not fascinating to me anymore. My manager and didi noticed this. Meanwhile, a new branch was being opened. So they handed over to me the complete branch's keys. Trusting me, they asked me to take over the branch and handle the customer care part. I took the charge of the complete branch. One more customer care support center started in a new place to service the CDMA mobiles.

As the responsibilities increased, I started to service these mobiles. I still remember there is one complaint about a broken display and it was a very costly mobile. My manager asked me to replace the display. He walked me through the steps once and left. That was the first time I felt fearful while replacing the costly items. I was not sure whether I could do that because it had been a year since I held the solder gun which was taught by my teachers in my college days. What I had learned was soldering for bigger wires but, this time, the mobile display was very small, thin and extra care was required. We had to do it without causing damage to the important parts of the display.

However, I damaged one costly display. When my boss saw that, he got irritated because it had cost him. I was not happy with what I had done. That soldering and servicing part was very new to me and I did not like what I had done. I was very upset that day.

Paper Add mistake

The next day when I came back to the office, I saw an advertisement that relayed a job with a salary of Rs. 15000 per month. It caught my attention, and without thinking much, I said that I was not going to work there. I would join a new company that would pay me more than what I was earning then. Without asking about the nature of the profile, I simply left my current job and went to join there.

That was the worst decision I have ever made in my career. It was not a good option. They treated entry-level people as school students. In the first half of the morning, they made us stand in the queue to shout and clap. Later, we had to go to the field and pitch sales to the people who were willing to buy the SIM cards.

It was a road to hell. We had to promote the current offers of Sims and Sim company from pillar to post. As the company was new in the market, we were asked to close at least 15 deals/day, selling SIM cards, a vague method for me.

Then we had to collect the address proof and submit it back to the office. The salary amount depended on the number of sims you sold in that month. For me, it was a complete trap. I was not happy because I did not find a connection with that job.

My experience was not good. So, be careful of such types of advertisements or services that make you work and give nothing. I was foolish that I had left the monthly salary paying job and switched to the field where I had no experience in selling. It was very uncomfortable for me because it was not the technical one that I used to do. So, I was jobless again.

So, what is the learning from this experience? If you are looking for a job or planning to switch job, never assume that your new or next job will fulfill all your requirements. Be careful about your expenses and the kind of job you get. Always take a calculated risk and never jump to a conclusion without any verification. This is the biggest mistake that can cost you a lot. It is very difficult to get the monthly job back when you are not mentally prepared and especially when your pocket is empty. Therefore, be careful while taking any decision about your career.

At that time, I was sharing a room with my friend, paying rent for a sheet roof. I had to prepare my CV again and look for a job.

Adding 6 months of CDMA mobile repair experience to my CV, I started applying for jobs. As usual, the same story repeated. This time even worst as I used to take my CV from company to company, thinking that they will welcome me inside, take my interview and give me a job.

But it was not that much easy, because I was applying for the jobs inappropriately. I did not improvise my CV according to the interview. I never prepared for the interview and submitted the same CV everywhere. I even used –to ask the security guards of the companies to help me get a job (I was that mad).

After my misadventure at the last job, I was looking desperately for a new job. It translated into another struggle for 3 months. I was like a bag of bones, worried, frustrated and helpless. One day, as I was leaning on the carpet, I got a call.

The universe wanted me to do something else. My uncle called me and asked how was my job and if everything was fine.

I said to him I was not ok. I was not liking my last job because sales was not my forte. I had studied technical, so I am supposed to work on technical only. If I continue to work in sales, chances are that I may lose track of my technical skills and my future won't be good." That was what I thought at the beginning of my career.

What you can learn here is:

1. If you are working or going to work, before changing to a new job — have at least 6 months of the backup amount in reserve.
2. Never jump or switch without verifying the company and nature of the job. Do some research.
3. Keep a track of your progress.

4. Take calculated risks and seek advice before taking a major decision.
5. Mentally prepare for the new environment.

ACTIVITY 4

Keep one hand on your heart and the other on your mind and say:

"I am ready for my Dream Career"

"I am ready to succeed in "Passion, Career & Paisa"

"I am ready to see my new opportunities"

1. Write the mistakes that you can avoid at the onset of your career.

____

____

____

2. Write how well prepared you are for the new opportunities.

____

____

____

1.3.3 JOURNEY OF TRAVELING JOBS

Finally, I got a job that was very technical, Field service engineers were required all over Karnataka in the medical domain. The interview was at Chandigarh.

Therefore, I had to take a train from Bangalore to Chandigarh, which takes 45 hours. So it took me nearly one week to complete the interview.

Train to Chandigarh: Bangalore to Hazrat Nizamuddin Express- The local train started from Bangalore on

Day 1 - City Railway station - Andhra Pradesh.

Day 2 - Secunderabad, Bhopal (tried Hyderabadi biriyani).

Day 3 - Gwalior, Agra, Delhi (tried Agra ka petha).

I arrived at the Chandigarh railway station. Being a South Indian, I was visiting North India for the first time. It was a completely different look, people, road, food, etc.

Chandigarh - The City Beautiful - one of India's well-planned cities, the capital of the northern Indian states of Punjab and Haryana, was designed by the Swiss-French modernist architect, Le Corbusier.

As 45 hours of the journey was long and I was tired, so the first thing I looked for was room to lean my back on the bed. I walked out of the station and looked for autos (like in South India) but did not find one. Most of them were 3-wheeler rickshaws (cycle) or horse carts.

So I asked one person, "Bhaiya yahaan auto milega kya? (Can I get an auto here?)

He answered, "Nahin bhaiya - rickshaw se chale jao. (No, you can go by cycle rickshaw.)

"Oh," I said, "then pass mein accha hotel milega kya" (Is there any good hotel nearby stay?)

A rickshaw person overheard my inquiry, he came to me and said, "Baiya, aa jao, mein tume choad dunga. (Come, I will drop you.) And I agreed.

I loaded my luggage and the rickshaw man started to paddle. Then I checked the address, which looked very simple.

Chandigarh is a very well-planned and beautiful city.

The house/building number and the sector number; only these two are good enough. If you tell these, any person will immediately guide you.

I asked the rickshaw man to take me somewhere close to Sector 34, as my interview was scheduled there the next day at 9 am. I wanted to stay nearby and be on time.

If you don't know Hindi, it's difficult to understand Punjabi, as most Punjabis speak like this - Haan ji, sab vadiya hai! (Everything is good)

After resting for a few minutes, I could not resist seeing the city around. The same day evening, I went for an evening walk. It was cold out there, In Chandigarh, the summers are very hot and the winters too cold. Over the course of the year, the temperature typically varies from 8°C to 40°C. While walking on the street, I observed the wide-open roads, wide footpaths, each road with markings, sector numbers board at each corner, each area, park, no tall building, less population, perfect goal chakkar (circle with direction), greenery everywhere and evening lights. Wow, it's perfect to leave here, I said. It was for the first time I had noticed such a beautiful city in India.

While I was walking, the weather was getting cold. On a simple four-wheeler cart, I saw chicken soup for Rs. 10. I decided to slurp it. Wow, it was not much spicy, very hot, with ample chicken chunks and tasty. The quantity was good, so I didn't feel hungry that night and just went to bed.

The next day morning, I got up early and hired a rickshaw to reach the interview place. I was early by 30 minutes, so I decided to have breakfast. Chandigarh's specialty is that, unlike South India, they don't cook varieties of breakfast. So the only choice I had was - paratha and bread pakora.

I asked the hotel person, "What you have for breakfast?" He said, "Paratha hai, bread cake hai."

I returned, "Aur kya hai?"

He said, "Alu ka paratha, gobi ka paratha, mix paratha aur bread pakora."

Again, the same.

So, I decided to eat something and go.

Give bread pakora.

Normally, bread pakora is triangular, sandwiched, but an important point to notice is they apply flour atta to bread and they fry it before they serve.

I had seen this type of delicious dish for the first time. My mouth started to water. It was piping hot, but when I took the first bite, wow, it was so tasty.

I could not resist, so I had two of them.

It was now the interview time. I went to the office upstairs. There were pagdi uncles, Patiala salwar aunties, and a completely different environment.

I liked their dresses and the way they talked, hanji hanji.

I met the HR who took my CV and called the company MD.

I was told to sit in the meeting room. After a few moments, two well-suited, big personalities stepped into the room. Oops, I got nervous. But I was well prepared, well dressed, looking smart and had a fresher's CV in my hand, which was not so attractive but ok to present.

One of them asked for my CV and a conversation started with tell me about yourself.

The interview went on, and they were happy to take me as a Service Engineer for the Bangalore position.

Immediately after the interview, I was guided to meet the Service Head. So, I met him, he also asked a few questions and asked me to stay for one week for training.

De dana dan – I got my first technical job in the Medical Domain.

ACTIVITY 5

Keep one hand on your heart and the other on your mind, and say:

"I am ready for my Dreamwork"

"I am ready to succeed in "Passion, Career & Paisa"

"I am ready to face the world"

1. Write about your first career interview or meeting learning experience.

____

____

____

____

1.3.4 TRAVELING BECAME MY OBSESSION

You will never become who you want to be if you are so attached to who you have been.

My Karnataka darshan (journey) started here because the job demanded a lot of traveling. I had to run around all the districts of Karnataka.

After coming back to Bangalore, my manager asked me to come to the branch. It was in Rajajinagar. After dressing neatly, I took the bus from Srinivas Nagar to Rajajinagar.

9.30 am was the official time and I would reach at 9:15 am. So, I could have my breakfast nearby before entering the office. This became my daily routine. On the first day, when I was waiting at the office gate as it was closed, one fat guy came and opened the office. When he saw me for the first time, he asked me if I had come to meet somebody. I said no - I was joining there that day. He said he was the office boy. Then he said to me, "Nice nice, I take care of the office, I do that, I do this, you contact me, don't worry." He was very talkative, but I had to listen to him as I had no other choice. Then one madam came, she was fair, walked fast, looked very tough and well educated. She noticed me and gestured to the wait for the manager to come.

The manager came along with another manager, holding office bags and a suitcase as if they were coming from a big project or had done some work. Both sat in their room for a few minutes, talking about the calls they had finished. Then one of them said to me, "Come, meet Madhu and I am Nagesh. We take care of the entire Karnataka for service, and you will be part of this. You can get further details from Madhu.

And let's go for coffee/tea." While sipping tea, one of them said, "Look, it's a traveling job and I know that you got the basic training from the factory. So today, you go with Madhu to learn the servicing of equipment." I said, "Ok." They asked me to sit and complete the form with mam and order a toolkit for myself. A mail was sent to HR.

My Service in medical started with PMS - Preventive Maintenance Service. I slowly started learning all types of services with the support of my senior service personals. I am grateful to them as they always guided me in learning technical.

Six months later, I was doing a decent job. My dedication and commitment to my new manifesto and my obsession with staying self-motivated, rebuilding my life, and creating success for myself were paying off.

I started getting recognition in terms of higher training. The next levels of commitment started. Slowly, I got a grip on service, travel and my communications.

I visited Chandigarh thrice for higher-end trainings - got good scores in trainings as well.

Few engineers came into contact, supporting each other in case of any major breakdown and new high-end machine installations- it was a win-win situation in field services.

I had become the company's favorite Bengaluru service person. I was outperforming guys who had worked there for years, all of whom stood around scratching their heads, wondering what my "secret" was. They thought that I was blessed.

I knew plenty of people who started their careers and left hardmanship, which is required to be in the game for long, even if you face ups/downs in your career. The "secret" was that instead of being obsessed with horrible habits, I allowed myself to become obsessed with success with the same innocence and energy I had as a kid. Rather than denying my obsession with success, I gave myself permission to embrace it and started to get a taste of how life could be. I was making money for the first time and saving all of it. More importantly, for the first time in years, I felt good about myself.

My self-esteem was returning. I started to find my swag and belief in myself again. Though it was a long way to the kind of success I had dreamed of, I finally knew I was headed in the right direction.

1.3.4.1 Surprise Package at Conference Hall

Some journeys were amazing, and I tasted varieties of food. I was learning different types of communication, which means the North Karnataka food and language are different from malnad Karnataka food and language.

Each time I visited a new place - I was amazed by the lifestyle. It is so different in different districts in Karnataka.

My hard work created an opportunity.

Surprise Package at Conference Hall (Traveling all over India)

I was lucky enough to get medical conferences in Bangalore after long years. I was in the stall for installing machines that were going to represent the company brand in front of the stall.

1.3.4.2 India Darshan

My funda to work in jobs was when you give more to the company - the company will pay you more in return. I never calculated time or work when I started working.

The Bengaluru International Exhibition Center installed a high-end machine to display an event under IRIA (India Radiology Imaging Association) in India. The conference every year represented the main cities of India. This time, it came to Bangalore. I got the chance to work at a conference.

Many Indian and international companies came to participate, demonstrating their strengths and technology.

It was a prestigious chance for me to participate in that conference. Before the conference, the backend team's responsibility was to prepare the stage and demo equipment. Installing heavy and high-end machines was not an easy task. That night, it was very cold out there. Shifting the machine, arranging things and making it presentable for the next day was the task for that night. The machine got delivered late, and only a few hours were left to install it at the stall and prepare it for the morning.

At 10 pm, the machines shifted and were transported to the stall using cranes. After machine installation, only the outer stall can be prepared for banner and display. So I had challenges installing machines in only 5 hours, whereas the actual time required was double. Therefore, I got the team on the job and without thinking much, started the work. I managed to install and made the impossible task possible with dedication and plan. My team did a fantastic supporting job. This was appreciated by my managers and seniors. The next day's conference started at 8 am, and the stall was ready for demonstrations.

My team members were happy about their efforts. But there was someone watching me closely. He was the opposite stall's manager who was inspired by the day and night work.

After 3 days of the conference, I got a call from that manager who is looking for an engineer.

So I appeared for the interview and cracked it. Importantly, the company offered double the salary, and I also got the chance to visit SPAIN for training.

1.3.4.3 Spain Story!

तमन्ना था दिल में कुछ कर दिखाने का
(I had a desire to do something)
प्यास बड़ी थी आगे बढ़ने का
(I was hungry to move forward)
कभी जिम्मेदारी ने रोका कभी नहीं लोगों ने टोका
(Sometimes responsibility stopped me, sometimes people)
अब नहीं रुकूंगा क्योंकि जिंदगी में नहीं मिलता है बार-बार यह मौका
(I will not stop now because the opportunities do not strike again in life.)

— *Akhilesh Telkar*

For the first time ever, I was traveling by air. Yes, I am the first person in my family to take an airplane. It sounds common nowadays but back in 2008; it was an amazing experience for me because I had never gone to AIRPORTS. But this time, I was taking a flight, that too an International Flight to Spain.

I was excited when I was applying for the Schengen VISA. The interview, the passport process, the flight tickets, everything was a wonderful experience.

First time at the dinner table:

I Googled how to sit at a dinner table in foreign countries. Are there any table manners to follow?

We entered a beautiful Spanish multi-cuisine hotel and sat at the table.

There were two knives on the left, a spoon and fork on the right, a small designer plate at the center and two big kerchiefs (one in white color and the other one green).

Not sure which one was for what.

I was curious to see what others were doing because I did not want to appear weird in front of them.

Suddenly a waiter came in, "What do you like to have today?"

I said, "What?"

She repeated, "Aqua, beer or wine?"

Aqua was a new word to me, so I was not sure what to reply.

Beer - I had never drunk before.

Wine - I had heard that it is good for health.

So I was confused and had trouble making a quick decision, as others were waiting.

I said, "Wine."

OMG, for the first time in my life, I had to drink alcohol. So, I prayed for myself, God forgive me.

Drinks came and were served on the table.

I acted as if I drank a lot.

Had a first sip - Oh gosh- how bitter it was, how people drink bottles together!

My acting then continued for some time.

It was now food time.

Again, the waiter asked, "What you like to have in the main course?"

What? The main course, starters - all these terms were new to me.

The only fear I had this time was that I should not order something which I can't eat.

So I took a guess and said -chicken.

I eat very less, max to max two or three small pieces.

Guess what – the attender bought a big boiled chicken weighing at least 1kg.

Immediately I said, "I can't eat this much. Can you reduce the quantity please?"

Everyone around started seeing at me as if I had committed some crime.

Then one Spanish guy who had visited India understood my problem.

He said, "Akhilesh, you can eat how much like to. Rest leave it."

"Oh, ok," I said and then tried to eat at least a quarter of it.

The dinner got over and I was back to my hotel.

I felt very thirsty because I could see everything on the table except water.

So, I immediately searched for the new name - what is this Aqua?

I came to know what I was looking for was water!

Aqua means water, oh gosh!

The next day, I was confident about the order.

This time, again, the waiter asked, "Aqua, Beer, Wine?"

With hot-off-the-fire confidence, I said, "Aqua."

Now she asked, "Gas or no gas."

Oh gosh, not again!

Now what to say?

Fumbling, I said, "Gas."

I was looking for water to drink but it was not what I was served.

This time, it was soda.

Lesson learned:

If visiting outside your zone, do some homework, try to understand their culture, get familiar with language, and basic words.

Here are some learnings I gathered from the European culture:

1. They care for nature, resources like water, trees - use only if needed urgently.
2. They are very discipline in terms of following traffic rules - they stop even on green signals if they see some pedestrians crossing.
3. They use technology well, for example, fast metro trains, use punching cards, buy tickets in queues, allow others to go first, care for the elders and respect for the outsiders.

I roamed almost all the places in Madrid, took plenty of pictures, followed map routes that were easy to follow, took metro travels, and more. I also visited the famous Bull Fighting at the Plaza de Toros Las Ventas, known as Las Ventas. It is the largest bullfighting ring in Spain. The next day when told the trainer and others that I saw the bullfight - everyone was surprised. It was a very memorable trip of my life because no one from our family has traveled outside of India. My family was proud of my first endeavors.

1.4 BRAND CAREER

Lately, I realized I was not wearing the right shoes to grab bigger opportunities. So, I made extensive improvizations to my CV that was suitable for the right job.

Here are 4 things you need to do before you get into a dream career:

1. Build Your Brand CV (as discussed)
2. Create your Cover letter and One-page Story

3. Highlight your Skills and the Project you have handled
4. Update all your social media accounts

If you don't know how to sell yourself better than others, then you can't position yourself in the market

If you can't position, you can't grab the opportunity.

Then how you will achieve Career Success?

Preparation for your future starts with Branding and Positioning well in the market.

When I say branding, it is about your presence on social media, CV outlook and maximum reach.

"Career is not something where you create a CV, apply for a job, start working. Career now in the digital world is all about creating your value and place in the market for yourself."

— Akhilesh Telkar

We live in a world where there are always dual voices to face. From childhood, our mind has been conditioned by these choices.

Good or Bad

Black or White

Yes or No

In or Out

Slow or Fast

First or Last

Dark or Light

Rich or Poor

When it comes to self-development, how much time do you spend in your daily routine for self-awareness? How much time do you spend with yourself in a day, and how many new skills have you acquired?

How many books have you read in the last 90 days? What is the time you have given to your health, relationship and wealth?

It is true that some of us are like live walking books, with our own powerful stories to tell. Each story is different and offers to learn from experiences. In the end, what matters is how much time you spend from the inside out.

You have to make a daily conscious effort to develop yourself to grow in life.

if you want to achieve your dreams, then you must make that extra effort every day, every minute.

Fear is the most dangerous enemy. It will block you every time and not allow you to grow.

Once I came across a question on Quora!

What is the Scope of Junior Engineers today concerning technology?

If I have to answer this differently, I would like to give a world view.

The world is running behind technology, research, medical advancement, entertainment, nuclear power, etc...

If you see, all the sectors are interconnected and purely depend on engineering.

Example:

Life → depends on doctor → doctor depends on technology → technology means engineering.

Try to relate to our daily life, there is no place where engineering is not there. Daily we need the internet, mobile, electricity, water, medical assistance, transport and so on.

So engineering has made its place in everyone's lives. Today, there is a boatload of career options in the domain of engineering.

You must choose the right segment to get maximum benefit in your career.

Here are 3 points to remember:

1. You don't need to wait for the 'so-called' perfect time to do the right thing.
2. It never arrives on its own. You have to take the initiative to make it happen.
3. Wonders can happen in your career when you pray effectively.

During this career

I am grateful to the company I worked for. The growth every year was outstanding. I learned about new products, entered the world of digital radiography and became an expert in this area. Each year it was 30-40% growth, A Certificate of Excellence for Outstanding Performance and Contribution in 2010.

I traveled all over India and additionally visited Spain thrice and Italy twice. For 10 years, I gave my entire career to this company.

For me, success is defined by my potential. I never look at my salary slips, promotions, office politics, position or selfless work toward growth.

My criterion was - is my progress happening, am I respected in that place - otherwise you don't have to push yourself where you are not respected.

Over the years, my maturity ripened. I am more confident than before. Getting a job is not a difficult task anymore. I know how to make things happen.

My assessment of my potential has changed over the course of my life.

Your potential expands and reveals itself over time as you discover more of what you are capable of. I realize now I always underestimated my potential. I believe I still do sometimes, yet I am aware that I have yet to operate from my full potential—and am on a discovery of what that might be. So far in life, it was about getting a job, getting pay cheques, calculating monthly expenses, taking loans - whole life pays for it.

However, something always bothered me, it was not enough. I was sure I needed change, but because of my family's responsibility, I was unable to change. I feel struck - just like a fish in the fishbowl. It doesn't have the extra space to swim, no freedom, no outside world to see. The fish never knows what's happening outside. So, I wondered, is this what life is all about? I was not getting the answers, no clarity, whom to ask, what to do.

Every time I thought about it, I felt frustrated with myself. Is this the career growth I am looking for? Why am I not growing? Where is the fault? How to solve this puzzle?

I knew something else needed to be nosed out. I love destinations because once I reach them; they teach me something new about my potential.

After working for 10 years in the same company, I started feeling like I was living in a comfortable zone. I was not doing well and needed something else. It was the time for a change.

1.4.1 Taste of Real Opportunity

Lazy will wait for the opportunity to come;
Smart people will create an opportunity.

Then came one opportunity, it was an IT-Service base company.

I went to help for an interview and learned about this new opportunity. I said, let me try for myself. And it clicked, they got me or I can say; I got heaven to live in. Earlier, I was full of complaints. I was working in an office where my potential was underestimated, and I was eager to see the new world. And this opportunity gave me wings.

I was appointed to create "India's First nuclear lab".

The first installation was in Bengaluru, it was great to be part of this prestigious project. During the 4 years of my tenure in that company, I understood the software, the company's climates, the new corporate world, and I tasted a new life.

I built a beautiful lab from scratch.

For that, I got the BEST PERFORMANCE AWARD in 2019.

I have always secretly believed I am capable of doing unbelievable things. Even at the low points of my life, I had an understanding that my potential was greater than my achievements.

I worked under superman Mr. Chetan Chandrashekar, learned a lot of lessons from him, and met a few experienced and wonderful colleagues.

But the universe has some other plans. I was back at the same point where I started my career.

My first job was in Sales, and I was back in Business Development.

While in the BD team for 1 year, we did bring a few clients in. I didn't learn about closing clients here, but my basics about sales got super corrected.

One day, my boss called and informed me about the merger between two big giants. The change in management position affected the entire sales team.

That was a major shift in my career- that day's call shook me enough to think of something else immediately.

It's not just a career, it's your lifeline

— Akhilesh Telkar

No one is born with all the talent that makes an expert. Skills are something you develop over time and grow. Contrary to what we were told our entire lives, we are not born with our talents; we develop them. The ability to succeed in your career or anywhere else is not an innate talent, it's the mindset and lifestyle you adopt.

You may not feel like you have it in you just yet, and that's perfectly fine. Where you are today is not where you are going to stay. You still have a journey ahead of you, and this book is the first step toward realizing your talent. If you give yourself some time, if you invest in yourself and if you take action, you will get there. You will become super talented, no matter what your caretakers and so-called well-wishers think of your ambitions.

"Know Your Purpose, Find Your Passion and See Your Worth."

— Akhilesh Telkar

Some of the tactics in this book may cause your friends or loved ones to raise a brow. It may seem excessive, over the top, or simply ridiculous that you should spend time- a lot of time- on becoming a better version of yourself. When I first started focusing on career development, my family and friends thought I was losing it. They didn't understand what I was talking about when I mentioned how I was working on my limiting beliefs and visualizing my goals. They thought everything I was doing to upgrade myself was weird. I admit it was different. It wasn't what everyone else was doing, but that was the whole point.

You read this book, but if you don't believe in yourself, no matter how tactical the advice I share, if you don't think you can become successful, you probably won't become one. Now it's not about what other people think, it's about what you believe. Everyone around you may think you don't have what it takes and they will be wrong, but if you don't believe you have it in you, you will be right.

"What you believe, You Achieve."

— Akhilesh Telkar

Unfortunately, most people don't believe they can become successful. They wake up every morning, go to a job they hate, fill their time with endless distractions, and go home with a pay cheque, feeling sorry for themselves. It's not that they don't have the potential to become successful, because they do. What they don't realize is that they have all it takes to be successful.

You have picked this book because you want to be different, you want to do better and become the best version of yourself. You know you are meant for more, and this puts you ahead of most people. Let me tell you, being successful is an amazing feeling. You feel like a real-life superhero who is capable of doing the most incredible things. And this feeling keeps you motivated.

A DUSTED CAR

Two ladies who lived in the neighborhood gathered in front of their houses for their routine chinwag.

A dusted neighbor's car was parked on the roadside.

Looking at the car, they found their topic of discussion.

1st lady: Look at the car, a thick layer of dust rests on it.

2nd lady: Yes, it looks like has not been used for a long time.

1st lady: The owner of this car used to clean it every day.

2nd lady: Probably, he is in the town.

1st lady: No, maybe he has lost interest in cleaning his car every day.

One kid came and heard the two ladies' conversation. He then observed the car, which had many names and drawings carved on it.

Kid (in a confident tone): It seems like uncle is not interested anymore in tidying his car, so people have taken up this task by writing.

The kid's words may sound funny but there is a meaning alloyed.

"Life is like this only; don't stand in one place and allow the dust to gather. If you don't move or don't take action, people start writing on you like in the dusted car case. So, keep moving, keep fighting and keep trying.

— Akhilesh Telkar

Every day is a new day; find your purpose and passion. Please don't allow yourself to become tainted; otherwise, someone else will start to control (write) on you.

"Be your own self, make a difference,
and live a beautiful life."

— Akhilesh Telkar

1.5 CAREER ROAD MAP

Before You Build a Career, Build a Strong Character

Do you remember the common roadmap shared earlier? (Career road map: fig. 1)

It is now time to upgrade your career road map to Find "U" in "YOU" Road map.

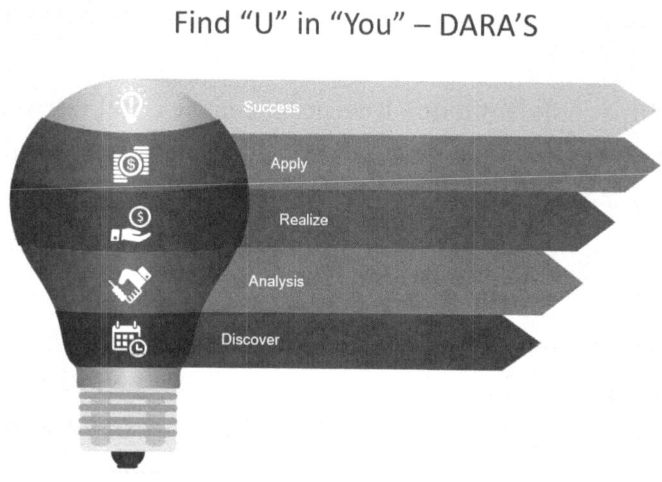

Career Find "U" in "YOU" Road Map1 : fig3

Find "U" in "You"

1. **Discover- Where to Go?**

   Before you choose your career, decide where to go

   Check your interest, check your subjects

   Find your passion, know your purpose

2. **Analyze- What to do next?**

   Introspect to understand, choose what is right for you

   What naturally attracts you, spend time in this domain

3. **Realize- Which route to take?**

   Know your calling, match your path

   Power up your belief, take the leap of hope

   Match your skills, select your path

4. **Apply- Whom?**

   For whom you are doing, Yourself/Family/Society

5. **Success- When?**

   Know when you are fully aware, clear your limiting belief

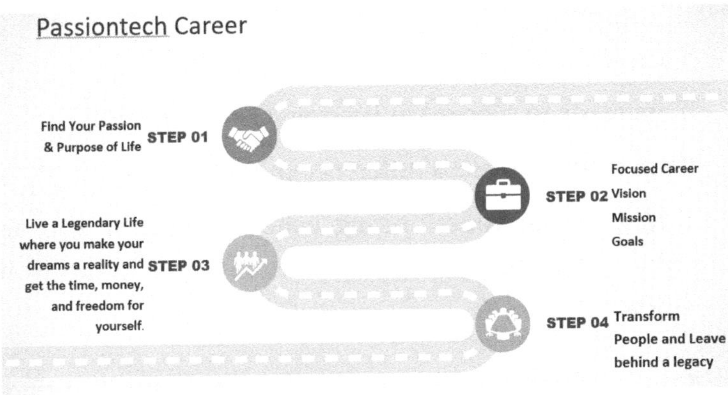

Fig4 : Career Find "U" in "YOU" Road Map2

Your career road map starts much before you think and must end with you leaving behind a legacy. In the above diagram, see the road has started very early and continues even after you are not present.

Remember we discussed earlier about childhood conditioning, the choices our caretakers make and how we get influenced by our surroundings?

So, here are the 4 steps to kick-start your journey:

Step 1 : Find your passion and purpose in Life

Step 2 : Focused career approach - Vision, Mission and Goals

Step 3 : Live a legendary life where you transform your dreams into a reality and enjoy the time, money, and freedom for yourself

Step 4 : Transform people's lives and leave behind a legacy

ACTIVITY 6

Keep one hand on your heart, the other on your mind and say:

"I am ready to build my Brand Career"

"I am ready to succeed in Passion, Career & Paisa"

"I am ready to make a difference in my life"

1. Write about your limiting beliefs. Whatever you are doing, ask yourself where it takes you after 3 years from now.

____

____

____

2. Write 3 strengths that can change your career.

____

____

____

The upcoming chapter on passion can help you to identify your real potential.

CHAPTER 2

PASSION (POLYTECHNIC TO PASSIONTECHINIC)

2.1 NOW IT'S TIME FOR CHANGE

"People become extraordinary when they have extraordinary Dreams. Make small changes every day, i.e. 1% Change per day. Now in 1 year, you have 365% changes."

~ Akhilesh Telkar

Have you ever asked yourself what's your passion?

Let's deep dive into the chapter to understand how this affects our careers.

2.1.1 Career Struggles Without Passion

What you are today is because of your yesterday's decision.

The majority of people do not want to take the headaches that come with starting their own business, but would rather follow instructions from others obediently.

I too was a follower at one time.

We all are natural leaders. You too have the ability to delegate tasks and make decisions.

However, most of us choose others to lead us. Back then, we won countless prizes and activities every year. How does our talent change as we grow and gain responsibilities? It was once easy for us to win games for the team, and be fearless on stage, in drama, dance, singing and sports. But as we grow older, we lose sight of those things.

We end up being in a materialistic world without passion.

Life should not be an unopened package, do everything the way you are.

What was missing in my life? I was struck at one level, thinking about what was next. I couldn't go forward because of my limiting belief system.

Alone only you can loan!

I was unclear about my life's path and what I wanted to accomplish. Those days in my career were scary. I was living a meaningless life, worrying about my monthly pay cheques. I was always scared about what will happen if I one day lose my job, what will I do to earn my daily bread and how will I provide for my family? What if I don't receive a salary raise? What can I do to increase my chances of improving my quality of life? Instead of seeking fulfillment, I was chasing success.

I spent almost half of my age doing jobs, roaming and working for someone else's goals. Actually, I was trading my time for money.

Here are the elements I was missing:

1. No clear vision
2. No future plans
3. No time
4. No clarity about life
5. No positive mindset

My biggest mistakes were:

1. Trading my time for money
2. Relaxed approach - wasting time
3. No self-development, mediocre mindset
4. Unhealthy habits
5. Ignored family life

2.1.2 Unsuccessful attempts

"Your Income will never grow until your personal growth starts:

I- Inner-strength,

N- Natural leader,

C- Cult,

O- Overcome Fear,

M- Motivation,

E-Energy."

— Akhilesh Telkar

As mentioned earlier, we tend to listen to society and get influenced by what's running around. We try to do the same as our loved ones do most of the time. However, most of the time, we keep struggling with our finances.

Here are some good investment options I came across:

1. Buying Gold - saving for emergencies
2. Policy Bonds
3. Mutual Funds
4. Crypto investment
5. Share market

But, if observed that saving for rainy days is a long-term game, and you need money to make money.

In difficult times, Don't say Why me? - Say Try me.

ACTIVITY 7

Keep one hand on your heart, the other on your mind and say:

"I am ready to solve problems"

"I am ready to succeed in Passion, Career & Paisa"

"I am ready to defeat my challenges"

1. Write on priority what are the problems you like to solve in your career.

   ____

   ____

   ____

2. Write the biggest challenges you are facing in your career right now.

   ____

   ____

   ____

2.2 Passion - Running water faces more challenges

"First things first
I'ma say all the words inside my head
I'm fired up and tired of the way that things have been, oh-ooh
The way that things have been, oh-ooh
Second thing second
Don't you tell me what you think that I could be
I'm the one at the sail, I'm the master of my sea, oh-ooh
The master of my sea, oh-ooh
I was broken from a young age
Taking my sulking to the masses
Writing my poems for the few
That look at me, took to me, shook to me, feeling me
Singing from heartache from the pain
Taking my message from the veins
Speaking my lesson from the brain
Seeing the beauty through the...
Pain!
You made me a, you made me a believer, believer
Pain!
You break me down and build me up, believer, believer
Pain!
Oh, let the bullets fly, oh, let them rain
My life, my love, my drive, it came from...
Pain!

You made me a, you made me a believer, believer" (Credit to Imagine Dragons)

This Believer song from Imagine Dragons was playing when I joined an online webinar on 2nd Jan 22.

I was trying out an app to trade money instantly using a graph. Sometimes you get good results, and sometimes you don't. I was trying to figure out another way to make money! I also saw an advertisement every day when I opened my YouTube channel. Being a person who is always eager to learn new things and looks for answers that have not been answered for so long, this offer caught my attention and I decided to enroll.

In fact, I was so frustrated and, in a hurry, to know "Why Rich people get Richer and Poor are still Poor".

So, I enrolled in two Rs. 99 webinars for the same date. And on the 2nd of January - do you believe that I paid Rs. 20,000 each for both the programs for the next level 3-day master classes without thinking much?

There is Just and there is Adjust

The webinars were all about the present status and where you would like to be in the future. The first webinar was scheduled for Sunday morning and the second on Sunday evening. The first one was more about business acceleration - and I enrolled for the next 3 days' master class- I was desperate to grow.

In the second webinar, the process was quite promising, so I decided to take up the next level 3-day master class for this program as well.

The first 3-day master class was supposed to wrap up in 15 days immediately after enrolling. The classes were good but to go to the next level; they were asking for a fee that was in lakhs. So, I decided to check out the other master's class.

After enrolling in the second one, I got access to university courses like how to find your passion, how to think and grow rich, how to write a book, and a few other courses. Access to FB, WhatsApp allowed me to connect with their community. This kept me engaged for 4 months until 08 April 22.

The most wanted day had come. I was in a 3-day master class.

It was all about why, what, who and when- finding your purpose, passion and getting more clarity of the future on vision, mission and goals.

It also included:

— Finding your idea, clarity, skills and what problem you can solve

— High-income skills, Program building, Product and Services, Funnels

— 3 Levels of Investment

— Investment in Self

— Business Investment

— Passive Investment

I was so involved and it encouraged me to take higher-level training.

Day 1 - 3 pm: Application form sent for next mentorship program

Day 2 - 8 pm: 1 lac paid (even if you pay, still there is a qualification process)

Day 3 - 10 am: looking for my name to be announced on the screen

No Name - Heart just broken, Dreams Shattered, Fear of going back to ignorance...

"Fear of losing value is much bigger
than losing money in the game of Life."

— Akhilesh Telkar

Tears filled my eyes, I felt as if my future was over.

I started thinking about what had gone wrong,

But I said to myself- If you have to earn yourself something, you need to show up better than what you are...

I started talking to myself– Akhi, have patience, it's a process... everything happens for the good. There were so many things playing in my mind. I was not worried about money, rather, I was fearful about my future like who will guide me further and how I can continue in my career from here. I was enveloped in so many negative thoughts. Holding my mobile, I started staring at the blank screen.

Guess what - a WhatsApp message popped up.

"If you are seeing this message, then your interview is scheduled at 9 pm."

I again started feeling hopeful about getting qualified for the mentorship program.

Fatha sir was my interviewer.

Day 3 - 9:25 pm: Discussion started, During the interview, I poured my heart out by sharing the entanglement I found myself in.

My humble gratitude to the community and on Day 3 - 11:59 pm: I received a team mail - Approved for PPMM8 batch...

I hoped to see new rays of life and was proud to be a part of the PPMM8 batch.

Thank you, Dev Guru.

Next case study meri hoga (the next case study will be mine).

2.2.1 "Courage is like a Muscle"

"Courage Is Doing Small Things
Step By Step To Make It Big."

— Akhilesh Telkar

My decision was big and impactful from all angles - family, career, and growth, and I had not told anyone about it.

However, one thing I knew was that I had made the best and toughest decision of life: Investing in "Myself":

- For Growth, I Need Self Education...
- For Business, I Need Money…
- For Happiness, I Need all the above...

Imagine if you don't have any of these now.

I often found myself in the quest of finding answers to many questions, like:

- How to Start?
- How to play a longer game?
- What can I do on priority today that will be fruitful tomorrow?
- Without investing?
- How to get famous and successful without money?
- What if my job and income are in danger?
- How to take a gut on investing in self-development?
- What is the plan B if my investment in self-development turns into a misadventure? How to bounce back?
- How do I know I am investing in the right place?

FEAR : F- Face E- Everything A- and R- Rise

Fear kills more dreams than failure ever will."

— Suzy Kassem

There were important areas of my life that needed immediate repairs at that time:

1. Self-Discovery
2. Finding Purpose/Passion
3. Career Road Map
4. Business Road Map

I got a signal that if I don't start changing now, then when? It was a now or never situation.

ACTIVITY 8

Keep one hand on your heart, the other on your mind and say:

"I am ready to discover myself"

"I am ready to succeed in "Passion, Career & Paisa"

"I am ready to invest in self-development"

1. What is the biggest investment you have made in yourself so far?

____

____

____

"Be ready to change with the change or be ready to perish under the change."

— Akhilesh Telkar

After completing the 3-day course, it was time to arrange the rest of the money, which was Rs. 4.5 lacs.

दिल में डर था, (There was fear in the heart)

आंखों में नमी, (Tear in the eyes)

चिंता किस बात की, जब मंजिल दूर नहीं (Why worry when you are close to your destination)

10 April 22 - 3 am: I was unable to sleep that night, trying to think and figure out how to arrange the rest of the money.

11 April 22 - 11 am: Until this time, my excel sheet was filled with some data.

Even if I liquidated all my FDs, MFs and CCs, I was still falling short of Rs. 1 lakh, which had to be paid before 17 April 22.

12 April 22 - 8:35 am: I got ready to visit the post office and withdraw my term deposit. However, upon reaching, I found that there was some issue with the passbook, so the officer told me to wait for 10 days for a new passbook. So I got stuck!

12 April 22 – 6 pm: High ticket closed gharme (at home).

Then ensued the conversation between me and Akka (my sister).

Me: Who is the first person from our family to fetch high marks in SSLC (Secondary School Leaving Certificate examination)?

Akka: You.

Me: Who is the first person to start working at 16 years of age and travel all over India?

Akka: You.

Me: Who is the first person in our family to take an international flight and travel to 3 countries?

Akka: You.

Me: Has anyone from our family written any book?

Akka: Hmmm, I guess not, why, what happened?

Me: How about I becoming the First Author in our family?

Akka: Her eyes widened in amazement. She started looking at me... (She had already noticed my social media presence and a few posts).

Me: Has anyone thought about this?

Akka: No, if you can, then it would be great!

Me: Then arrange Rs. "1lac" – haha.

Akka: Shocked and blank…

"The Universe doesn't give you what you want, it will give you when you deserve it."

— Dev Gadhvi

In 17 years of my career, for the first time, investing 4.5 lakhs for self-development to live my passion was not an easy decision. My inner voice was looking for answers.

As I have been working in Bangalore, from the beginning of my career to till now, every time I see big houses, fancy cars, rich lifestyles and successful people, I get fascinated and ask myself:

"Why Rich people get Richer, and Poor remain Poor?"

How could I reach that level where I am super-rich?

What is it that I should have done in the past or do now?

How soon will I be able to reach that position?

My inner voice always told me that it was possible and I could do it. But we often get influenced by people around us and circumstances. So, we start to deject and fail to convince our inner voice.

Being the best employee for the company I worked for, I always focused on a growth-oriented mindset.

However, I realized that working for long hours does not solve the problem.

Being not happy with the current situation and not thinking or not trying is a crime because it kills your dreams.

I wanted to be successful, but where to find the answer was a big question. I was trying hard, but in the wrong direction.

If you swim against the flow of the water, most likely, you will not reach your destination faster.

ACTIVITY 9

Keep one hand on your heart, the other on your mind and say:

"I am ready to remove negative beliefs"

"I am ready to succeed in "Passion, Career & Paisa"

"I am ready to face any fear"

First, write this on a piece of paper:

1. My idea is that 'I can't' do my work
2. I can't become successful
3. I can't make money
4. I am not great like others

Take this paper to a safe place, burn all these limiting beliefs or tear it into pieces and throw it into a bin.

Now write again all the beliefs that empower you:

1. I can do it
2. I am born to succeed
3. I am a money magnet
4. I am a legend

5. Through the days and nights, I am prospering in all my interest

Paste this on your daily sitting place or where you see it every day.

Proactive	Re-Active
Consistent in taking actions	Takes action only when required
Takes decisions on his/her own	Seeks others' approval while taking a decision
Considers learning as an investment	Sees learning as expenses
Takes Challenges	Fears taking challenges

You have two choices, which one would you like to choose:

1. ***Take the decision and make it right!***

OR

2. ***Wait for things to happen automatically!***

Fail Fast - It's better to take action today instead of waiting in the wings. Fail today by taking action for the betterment of the future instead of regretting later. You never know what winning story is waiting to unfold...

2.2.2 When you are looking for guidance in your life and Guru appears!

This is a scene from Mahabharata; the battle between Kauravas and Pandavas, where all men gathered young men, older men, brave men, leaders, and followers. As men entered the battlefield, they were unaware of the pain and destruction that was about to ensue.

As the battlefield was getting ready, Arjuna, led by Krishna, entered on his chariot. Arjuna taps on Krishna's shoulder and asks him to take him to the middle of the battlefield, saying, "I want to stare them down, lock eyes with them, scare them before grinding them into the dust."

Krishna chuckles, "Show off."

Arjuna - Can't help it; I am the most excellent archer in the world, can I?

Krishna - Ok, athmasarathi!

Steering the chariot in a direction and turning to look at the battlefield, he says, "All Yours. Stare away."

While standing in the middle of the battlefield, Arjuna witnesses something he had never seen before.

He sees roaring, hungry, impatient warriors, ready to fight, but they were all whom he recognized as fathers, grandfathers, brothers, and childhood saathis (friends).

The uncles, cousins, elders, and teachers who were a significant part of his childhood scolded, pampered, advised, and praised him for all the good deeds he received. They were all his family members who once spent time with him, studied with him, and laughed with him.

Arjuna was there to stare them down before he let his unerring arrows cut them down. Suddenly, the enormity of what he was about to do struck him like a thunderbolt. The most excellent archer in the world broke into a cold sweat. A deadly fear he had never encountered before paralyzed his mind. His knees buckled under him, and his hands shook uncontrollably, letting the Gandiva (bow) slip from his grasp.

Arjuna sobs, "I cannot do this? No, I can't."

Krishna was surprised! He asks, "What you cannot, Arjuna, what happened?"

Arjuna utters while pointing his arrow toward the Kaurava's army, "The war, the bloodshed, the killing, everything.

They are not my enemies; the enemy can't be my friends, relatives, and close family.

How can I fight and kill my near and dear ones? I cannot see my brothers in blood, and who I am trying to please? Bloody sacrifice? What sin can be greater than fratricide unless it is the sin of murdering your teacher?"

Krishna understands that Arjuna has lost his vision of being in battle. So, Krishna tries to convince Arjuna, "Why don't you understand that the opposite side also wants the same; they want to kill all and conquer the kingdom?"

Arjuna pleads, "I can't; I would rather die in battle. I can't kill my family members."

Krishna lips, "Come on, you know what this war was about; there is a family behind you that you need to lead to victory. This is disgraceful behavior for a warrior; you know there is no honor in running away from the battle, and dejection does not suit you."

Looking at Arjuna's face, he continues, "The greatest archer in the world who calls himself noblest of all warriors, destroyer of foes, most single-minded of men is now reluctant to fight!" He asks Arjuna to stand up, pick up the bow, fight with potential, do his duty, and fight the battle for Pandava's people as a prince.

This time, Arjun looks into the eyes of Krishna and regains his consciousness. Arjuna does what he had always done over the years in such situations. He turns to his closest friend and his wisest 'mentor', the only one he could trust; he listens carefully to Krishna and gets convinced of what he was supposed to do and obeys the Guru's path.

The rest is history.

Krishna guides us to do our duty with a single-minded focus and great sincerity, without worrying about the fruit.

"Man is made by his belief. As he believes, so he is!"

— Bhagawat Gita

Who is your biggest influencer, guide, or mentor in your career?

Call/message/email and say thank you to them for everything you have achieved.

Say thank you for......

Say thank you for......

Say thank you for......

2.2.3 How I found my Guru!

During the initial days of my career in Bengaluru, I used to spend Rs. 10 per meal.

Today my son eats pizza worth Rs. 1000, without thinking about what he is eating.

In my childhood, my mother used to buy groceries by saving little by little. Each month she used to take credit and pay the bill in the next month. That time, I was worried about our situation and used to think twice before spending even 50 paise.

After long years of my career journey, I had been thinking of starting an additional income, so that we had other sources to rely on.

I was watering the idea of starting a small business for a long time. So, I invested in the retail business. I said to mom that there was no need to think about groceries for home now, pick anything from the shop and cook.

I had my nose close to the grind but didn't understand why I was not growing.

In the quest to grow my business to the next level wondered what I was missing, and if was in the right direction.

Then, in 2022, I got the answer - the missing element was a "Guru".

When your vision is clear, then you are clear.

When you are clear, the student will appear.

When you appear as a student, the Guru will appear.

When the Guru will appear, everything is clear.

I am sure you know this - if you pray with good intentions, your prayer gets answered, no matter how, but you will surely feel the difference.

There was a time when I was struggling in the domain of finances. I did not know how to go to the next level. I was busy calculating and thinking about how I could change my status:

- Where can I get that abundance?
- Why do I have to go to work every day?
- Why am I doing all of these, where am I heading?
- What is the meaning of my life?
- Why am I born here?
- What is the one thing which I can do that people remember me for?
- How should my family remember me?
- How do I want my organization or employees to remember me?
- How do I want friends to remember me?
- How many lives do I want to impact in my lifetime?
- How should my kids remember me in the future?

Once I heard that we connect with people for some reason, people do not come into our life without reason... I connected too.

After the big loss of my dad, I was directionless, supportless and guideless!

No one was there to show me the right direction for my career. I thought that the only way to grow in my career was by working for companies, getting the hike and changing companies after some years. I was not sure whether I was fanning the right belief.

There was no one to tell me - this is the way to get success!

So many questions unanswered were reeling in my mind. That was the time when I came across the word “MENTOR”.

Only thinking didn't help, because I was not ready to pay to seek help from a mentor.

I missed my dad and often pondered what if my dad was alive when I went for graduation or even later. Would I be the same person I am?

Imagine if I had all the things that I wanted without asking, would I have put in this much effort to grow in life?

Such questions bothered me a lot. But one thing was sure that I was looking for someone who could answer all those questions.

So I thought of a few close ones to help me find the solutions. But then I thought- they may advise as per their understanding. I should ask these to an expert, one who knows the A to Z and has tasted success.

One day, I was sorting the things in my shop while listening to YouTube morning prayers. After that, every time I changed to some other video, one man used to appear and talk about the same thing that I was mostly looking for.

In one such advertisement, he was with his kid.

He asks his daughter Arianna - What you will do if you get 1 million rupees?

The 6-year-old answers - Hmmm, I will use this money to help poor people.

Dev answers back - No, if you use that money to help people - after it gets over, you will again end up with no money.

The first thing you should do is invest in yourself - Self-development is the key. If you don't know how to grow your money, again you will fail to maintain money.

Because the more you invest yourself, the more money you can make, the more money you make, the more people you can help, got it!

Wow, I said, yes, this is something I have been looking for.

Jindagi tu kaise karvaten badalti hai
(Hey life, how many shades do you have)

Kabi nami, kabi garmi
(Sometimes downs, sometimes ups)

Kaash kuch aisa hota sab kuch aasan hota
(wish there was a way everything was easy)

Kabi vo meri hota
(everything that is was mine)

Kabi ye meri hota
(everything this is was mine)

Kash har kuch meri mutthi me hota
(Wish everything was in my fist)

Are pagale, sab kuch itana asan hota
tho maza value ka thodi hota.
(Hey fool, if life had been that much easy,
success would not have been this valuable)

A teacher or lecturer is someone who can teach you and make you learn what is there in a syllabus.

A coach is someone who teaches you about a game or program, helps you reach the finals, and make it to the top of the game

Mentors are people who can allow you to unleash your potential and create the person you want to be.

What are the Qualities of a Good Mentor?

- Relevant expertise or knowledge
- Enthusiasm for sharing that expertise
- A respectful attitude
- Eagerness to invest in others
- The ability to give honest and direct feedback
- Reflective listening and empathy
- Willingness to be a sponsor

All of these play an important and equal role in everyone's life.

What are the 5 Cs of mentoring?

Five Cs: competence, character, confidence, connection, and compassion.

I wanted to be successful and help people to grow.

So I started investing in myself. One of the results of that investment is this book.

To begin with, let's find our present status, understand a bit, and find "U" in "YOU".

ACTIVITY 10

Keep one hand on your heart, the other on your mind and say:

"I am ready to learn"

"I am ready to succeed in Passion, Career & Paisa"

"I am ready to take the leap of hope"

1. Write the names of the ones you admire as your Guru. Call them or message them saying thank you for all the guidance they have given to you. List how you have changed after following their advice.

___

___

___

2.2.4 How to find your passion?

Most of the time, we get so unproductively busy in our day-to-day activities that we never think about the basic question: why am I here?

Have you ever asked, what's your purpose on this planet?

It is said that you are born twice on this planet - once when you are born and second when you know what's your calling and passion.

How to find your passion?

Identify the Problem, Know your Talent, Check the Market Demand

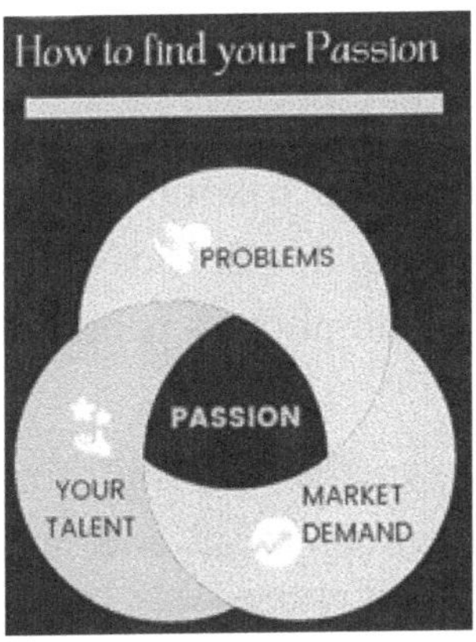

1. Is there something you already love to do?

Do you have a hobby or something interesting that you loved doing as a child, but never considered as a possibility for a job?

Whether it's reading comic books, collecting something, playing around or engaging in creative activity; chew over if there is something that piques your curiosity. If there's already something you love doing, you are ahead of the game. Now you just need to research the possibilities.

2. Find Out What You Spend Hours Reading About

For me, when I get passionate about something, I read about it for hours on end. I buy books and magazines. I spend days on the Internet finding out more.

There may be a few possibilities here for you, and all of them are possible career paths. Don't close your mind to these topics. Look into them until you feel your heart's content. This will help you get started as you learn how to find your passion.

3. Brainstorm

If nothing comes to mind right away as you are asking yourself how to find your passion, get out a sheet of paper and start writing down ideas. This doesn't need to be an organized list. It can simply be a paper full of random notes or even doodles.

Studies have shown that writing things down on paper points to better memory recall and leads to more robust brain activation.

Look around your house, on your computer, or your bookshelf for inspiration, and write down whatever comes to mind. There are no bad ideas at this stage. All of this will eventually come in handy later – they could be clues to the things you are passionate about.

4. Ask Around

There are likely people you admire in life, and there are things about them that you would like to replicate in yourself. Go to them if possible, and pick their brain. See how they landed where they currently are and whether they feel they've discovered their passion.

The more possibilities you find, the more likely your chances of learning how to find your passion in the long run. This may mean that you spend time talking to friends and family, coworkers, or even acquaintances in your free time. If you have a mentor, ask them if they have time to connect over coffee or lunch.

5. Don't Quit Your Job Just Yet (applicable to working people)

If you find your calling or your passion, don't turn in your resignation tomorrow. It's best to stay in your job while researching the possibilities.

If you can do your passion as a side job and build up the income for a few months or a year, that's even better. It gives you a chance to build up some savings (and if you are going into business for yourself, you will need that cash reserve) while practicing the skills you need.

6. Give It a Try First

It's best to test your new idea before jumping into it as a career, as you are wondering how to find your passion. Do it as a hobby or side hustle at first so that you can see if it's really your true calling.

You may be passionate about it for a few days, but where the rubber meets the road is the time to determine whether you are passionate about it for at least a few months.

If you pass this test, you have probably found it.

7. Do as Much Research as Possible

Know as much about your passion as possible. If this has been a passion for a while, you may have already been doing this. At any rate, do even more research.

Read every website on the topic and buy the best books available to live a more fulfilling life. Find other people, either in your area or on the Internet, who do what you want to do for a living, and quiz them about the profession.

How much do they make, and what training and education do they need? What skills are necessary, and how did they get their start? What recommendations do they have?

Often, you will find that people are more than willing to give advice.

8. Practice, Practice, and Practice Some More

If you are getting close to learning how to know your passion, don't go into it with an amateur skill level. If you want to make money or want to be a professional, you need to have professional skills.

Get very good at your future career, and you will make money at it. Practice for hours on end and learn how to focus; if it's something you love, the practice should be something you want to do and life fulfilling.

9. Never Quit Trying

It's possible that you won't be able to find your passion at first. However, if you give up after a few days, you are sure to fail. Keep trying, for months on end if necessary, and you will find it, eventually.

Perhaps you thought you found your passion, but discovered several months later that it wasn't for you. It's ok to start over again and find new parallels to passion. There may be more than one passion in your lifetime, so explore all the possibilities.

Lazy people always find new ideas to be lazy

Tracking your progress is another great way to reflect on your journey and see if there are adjustments that need to be made.

As per my mentor, passion should not be an expensive hobby. An important factor in everyone's journey is to understand and find missing elements, like knowing your purpose and passion.

Self-Potential → Identify your Skills → Know your strengths and weaknesses → Vision → Mission → Micro-niche → Clarity → Design your program → Future roadmap.

Steve Jobs said, "People with Passion Can Change the World."

There is no get-rich-quick formula.

Who wants to become Rich, Financial Free and Successful?

Everyone! Everyone! Everyone!

But why only a few achieve these and many struggle?

If you want to become successful, don't aim for success!

Yes.

Do you remember the movie 3 Idiots?

What Baba Ranchordas says?

"Success ke peeche mat bhago, Kabiliat ke peeche bhago. Success khud jhak marke piche ayegi."

— 3 Idiots

Nature has a fixed state, for example, a tree is rooted in one place. Trees don't have to be ambitious or will not say one day, "I will become the world's richest tree one day." But humans are not stationary. We aspire to be good humans, world-class, rich and successful.

80% of job workers are not happy because they don't have the freedom they want.

How many times have you wanted to become something, but cannot because of circumstances?

Another problem most of us suffer from is that things do not come easily to us, so they don't seem that amazing, and we dismiss them. Your superpower may not seem that big of a deal to you. It is something that comes naturally: something so simple that it couldn't possibly be that important. If you are an amazing cook, it may not be of much relevance to you. But for someone who cannot cook, it's a huge deal.

Maybe you are good at playing piano, fixing motorcycles, playing games, dancing, teaching, traveling or something else. Look at what comes easily to you and what you love to geek out on. Chances are that's where your superpower is hiding, just waiting to be developed and shared with the world.

So don't focus on changing the circumstance around you, first change yourself and see how the environment starts changing. When you instill changes in yourself, your perception of the world changes - See "U" in "YOU".

To go next level in life, you must think and act differently than the way you previously have been (10x Level as per Grant Cardone):

1. Growth mindset
2. More acceleration
3. Extra horsepower

Whenever I feel fearful of taking my next action step, it means I should take action.

Use fear to fuel your actions.

Quit your worries, build your career with passion, live a purposeful life and don't underestimate your potential.

"Success without fulfillment is an ultimate failure."

— Tony Robbins

ACTIVITY 11

Keep one hand on your heart, the other on your mind and say:

"I am ready to unleash my potential"

"I am ready to succeed in "Passion, Career & Paisa"

"I am ready to live a purposeful life"

1. Write problems you like to solve around.

___

___

___

___

2. Write the list of skills you have.

___

___

___

___

3. Research if your skills have a demand in the market place.

___

___

___

___

2.2.5 How did I Find My Passion?

Here are two incidents that happened to me before I was awakened to my inner calling:

It was 12.30 am, and everyone was sleeping. I was sitting outside the OT, and I could hear the screams of my wife.

When I looked at her through the glass, I could see the trauma in her eyes.

Restless, I would sit on the edge of the chair and then walk back and forth. As I saw the nurse, I asked her how much more time it would take. She said, any moment now."

Worried, I looked at the watch, it was 2:10 am. Suddenly, I saw the doctor brisking into the OT. I did not understand what was going on. The nurses started walking in and out with hurried steps. I could sense they were doing their best job in this world.

Then I heard something, a loud cry from inside OT. Oh God, the shriek was so thin, so innocent.

Now I was eager to see what was happening.

Then the nurse came outside and said, "Give new Cloth to Wrap."

Omg, I cannot express in words how relieved I felt. I saw my wife's face – she beamed a smile. I understood she was doing fine.

Then, I started informing my family members. The joy of happiness started flowing, everyone started jumping, dancing and shouting. That was the news everyone was waiting to hear.

"It is a Baby Boy."

Now, coming back to the point wherein the birth of my son transpired some magic.

Please re-read the above episode. What I have written is something that came naturally to me. Till that time, I had never written or planned to write. My son's birth triggered a spark in me to take up writing. What are the casual ways to inform about your baby's births?

Like everyone does when they have to inform the birth of their child, they type messages like:

Type 1: Blessed with a Prince/Boy or Queen/Girl.

Type 2: Pari, Jigar ka tukda, etc… Son/Daughter - Quite common to hear these, right?

As I wanted to inform all the close ones, so I typed the above message just like that. Now the point is, when I shared this with my loved ones, I was amazed to know another creative quality of mine: “Writing”.

My first realization eventuated at the time of my son’s birth time, which led me to the Framework “Find "U” in "YOU “.

Before he came to this world, gave me something miraculous that I was unaware of. It was 22 September 2016 when I came to know about this hidden quality of mine, but I forgot it after a few days.

My second realization was when I conducted a virtual meetup for our friends’ group. Our friends were feeling bored with their daily routine. They were looking for some change, and that virtual meeting gave them a boost to see their friends once again.

We wanted to connect and recall those good old memories. So 8 active friends from that group teamed up and started discussing their program schedule, sequence, videos, teacher’s surprise, chit-chat, etc.

When I was communicating with my friends during that chat, I noticed that I was sharing some amazing messages. Unknowingly, I was writing some poems, which my friends admired. But even at that time, I was unaware of this strength of mine.

Then in 2022, for the first time, I connected with Devguru, my Mentor, who ignited my Passion. My self-development journey with one of the finest mentor Anju Choudhry started.

I realized that writing is my Passion:

1. It comes naturally to me.

2. This is one thing which I can spend a lot of time and effort on.
3. I can add value to others' lives through my content.

Some more important factors:

1. Books help me connect with people to build relationships.
2. Even after I am gone, my books will stay forever.
3. If you ask me - what is the one thing I like to leave behind - its memories in the form of writing.
4. Writing helps me become a role model for my family.

Let's see what happened next and what else I discovered.

ACTIVITY 12

Keep one hand on your heart, the other on your mind and say:

"I am ready to follow my passion"

"I am ready to succeed in "Passion, Career & Paisa"

"I am ready to commit to my purpose"

1. Close your eyes and recall what interests you the most. Identify if that's your passion. Write all about the same.

____

____

____

____

Warning: Do not skip any exercise - I will share at the end of the book why it's important to write the answers.

2.3: FRAMEWORK ⟶ FIND "U" IN "YOU"

Find

F : Found ⟶ Discovery Stage

I : Imagine ⟶ Visualize your future

N : Nirvana ⟶ Sense of self

D : Deep Inside ⟶ Immerse yourself

"U" :

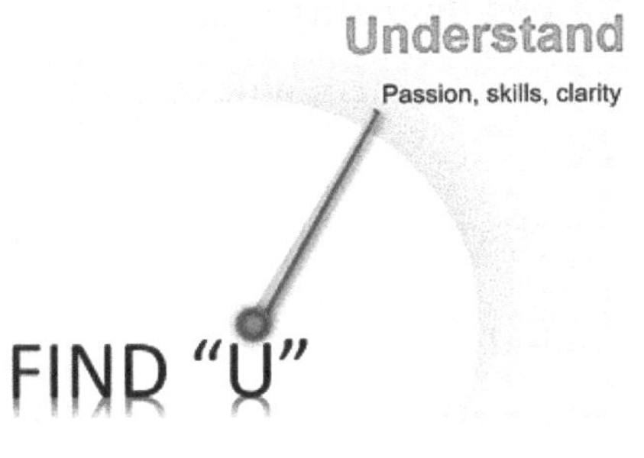

Understand ⟶ Passion, Skills, Clarity

IN :

I - Implement ⟶ Bring massive actions

N- Never give up ⟶ Build the courage muscle

"YOU"

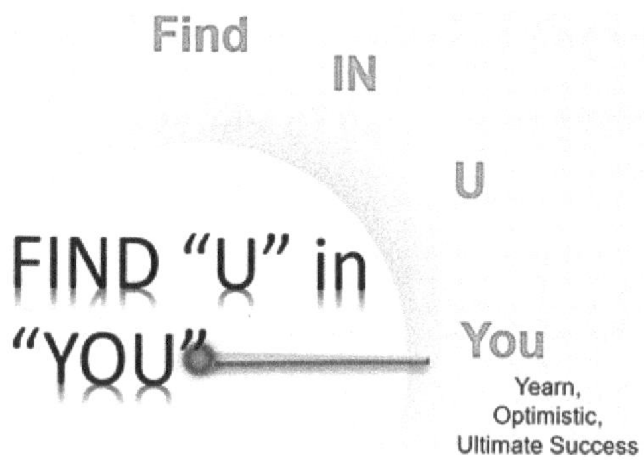

Y : Yearn ⟶ Strong desire to achieve

O : Optimistic ⟶ Confident and positive about what you are expecting

U : Ultimate Success ⟶ it's all you most wanted

2.3.1 Right Mindset

1. Right thinking
2. Desire to become
3. Feed the beast

5 signs that show you have a strong mindset:

1. You celebrate the success of others (you don't feel jealous and appreciate others' achievements).
2. You embrace change (you welcome new ideas, changes and are ready to face challenges).
3. You move on (you won't get stuck in one place, feel sorry and waste time > actually you take action and move on).
4. You stay positive even under pressure (you don't waste energy on things you can't control or things that drain your energy).
5. You aren't afraid to speak up (you don't hide your true intentions and go after what you want).

Start with Great Thinking.

Learning comes first, then earning follows.

Change your knowledge, thinking, choices, your vehicle (your mindset) and see the changes in the result.

The fact is that your character, thinking and beliefs are critical in determining the level of your success.

"The key to success is to raise your energy; when you do, people will naturally be attracted to you."

— Stuart Wilde

Technology has continued to influence—and even define—how people identify and procure employment. Increasingly, the job search has moved online.

Some people's choice of career is dictated by their passions. They simply have to create art, make music, or seek a cure for cancer. And certainly, we are all better off with our efforts. Other people are more pragmatic and give more weight to practical concerns when making career decisions. Regardless of what camp you fall into, all career seekers can benefit from looking down the road at the careers the experts predict will be most in demand in the future. With this in mind, we share some new information about a few important trends.

If you keep doing what you are doing, the result will be limited, so keep doing the right things at a higher rate.

2.3.2 Problems to solve

Articulate the problems well ⟶ Become a Problem expert

Your idea is not to be perfect, but it must solve a problem and be beneficial to others.

Look around, there are plenty of problems to address, including our own.

But if you are truly passionate about becoming a problem-solving expert, then start finding problems first. When you put your head to it, there are many ways to solve these problems, but the person who resolves them in a simplified way will always go ahead.

The best examples are stories of RED BUS, UBER, NO BROKER, etc.

They felt that pain, then put their mind into solving and the result is a successful business idea.

Identify the problem first ⟶ Check the skills you have ⟶ Research the Demand ⟶ Start work toward your brand career

2.3.3 Skills that can pay your Bills

There is an ocean of knowledge available, if you walk with a spoon, how will you fill it?

Don't look for a new job, look for a new skill to develop.

Your skills can pay more than your job.

Check how many books you read this year; check what new skills you have added to your basket.

"Better skills create more Opportunities."

Work hard on your job so you make your company proud.

Work hard on yourself so you can make your country proud.

Fortune brings joy.

Now you know how to start.

Start from the Heart ⟶ Bring Brains to it

List down the skills you possess, it may be anything that you love to do.

Good to Have Vs Must Have.

ACTIVITY 13

Keep one hand on your heart, the other on your mind and say:

"I am ready to upgrade"

"I am ready to succeed in "Passion, Career & Paisa"

"I am ready to solve problems using my skills"

List the skills:

1. That naturally come to you

2. That you are interested in
3. Which you think will solve others' problems
4. That are connected with your demand area

Example: Identify your category to start with

Health : Cooking, Fitness, Habits

Wealth : Finance, Investments, Money Management

Relationship : Personal, Family, Acquaintances

Career Development : Jobs, Skills-based, Solo or Entrepreneurs

Which one most suits you?

Cooking, Traveling, Dancing, Repairing, Writing, Speaking, Trainer, Self-image, Technical or Non-technical, the list goes on, anything which naturally comes to you.

Start assigning points to it - Check your expertise, how much score out of 10 can you slot?

Example:

Health ⟶ Yoga Expert-9 ⟶ Sports trainer-8 ⟶ Mindset Coach-8 = 25

Wealth ⟶ Financial advice-6 ⟶ Real-estate expert-7 ⟶ Accounts-8 = 21

Relationship ⟶ Parenting-5 ⟶ Childcare-7 ⟶ Life Coach-7 = 19

Career ⟶ Software developer-7 ⟶ Admin-8 ⟶ Designer-7 = 22

List the top skills- give the score for each skill out of 10- the first 3 with the highest score are what your heart and soul like.

You don't get what you want, you get what you deserve.

Do the above exercise regularly, and your skills are ready now.

2.3.4 Demand in the market place

Solve Complex problems of the market in a Simplest Manner

The below exercise helps you identify and know your market, especially the ones starting a new business.

Survey your environment, check on Google, check with your contacts, check your society, check your community - What is that most people are looking for?

Again, score each demand:

Local Demand → Local Supply

Local Demand → Global Supply

Local Supply → Global Demand

Global Supply → Local Demand

Now match them:

2.3.2, 2.3.3 and 2.3.4 -Revisit -do the exercise to know your passion:

1. Identify the pain and problems.
2. Match with the skills that you have.
3. Check how much demand there is in the marketplace.

And here you are with Passion in place, which you can drive throughout your life.

Now you can say that you have pretty much identified your passion, but still the important factor you need to address is "Micro-Niche".

There are four core markets or desires that are i.e., health, wealth, relationships and career.

When people purchase a product or service, they are hoping to get a certain result in one of these four areas of their lives.

Every product or service fits into one of these four core desires or markets.

So the first question you need to answer is this:

Which of these four desires are my future dreams match?

Only do it if it makes your life easier.

For most people, this is a simple question to answer, but sometimes, people get stuck for one of two reasons.

For example, in the domain of health, there are hundreds of ways to achieve a healthy state. You might want to do it by losing weight or gaining muscle. Similarly, if you want to be wealthy, you might want to do it through entrepreneurship or sole-preneurship. If you want to improve your relationships, you might need marriage advice or dating advice. The list of submarkets is practically endless in any of the core markets.

ACTIVITY 14

Keep one hand on your heart, the other on your mind and say:

"I am ready to win hearts"

"I am ready to succeed in "Passion, Career & Paisa"

"I am ready to be the number1 in the market"

So here is the next set of questions to ask yourself:

1. What are the other submarkets in demand that I can work for?

____

____

____

2. What is the submarket where my skills match my passion?

____

____

____

CREATING YOUR OWN CATEGORY (AND BECOMING THE CATEGORY KING)

2.4 SOCIAL MEDIA MASTERY

Before they buy your product, they should buy "You"

2.4.1 Content is the key

There is a famous saying; If you are not on social media, you do not exist in the world.

ACTIVITY 15

Keep one hand on your heart, the other on your mind and say:

"I am ready to see the true me"

"I am ready to succeed in "Passion, Career & Paisa"

"I am ready to change my status"

Take some tests:

Test 1: Google your name

What do you get?

If your profiles are not highlighting as per your expertise, then it is time to update all your social media profiles.

Test 2: Be true to yourself - check your YouTube history

What content you are consuming? You should focus on your area of interests like career-oriented, motivational, knowledge-based programs and your passion. If not, you know where you are heading!

Claim the spot.

Success is your responsibility. The bigger the commitment, the bigger the Success.

Become an Expert, Become the Number 1.

In my self-development year, I have solved numerous problems for myself and getting better every day.

By the time you read this book, the list may increase exponentially.

Problems Solved for My-self	Skills Developed
English communication	Content
Fear of presenting my-self	Social Media Mastery
Social media myths	Story Telling
Poor thinking about money	Branding
No clarity about life	Video Editing
Mindset	Website/Landing Page
VMG -Vision/Mission/Goals	Sales Funnels
Health Habits	1:1 Coaching
	Book Writing and Publishing
	Book Reading
	Leadership
	Poems
	Copy Writing
	Podcast
	Program building
	Project management

For the first time in my life ever, I made my own podcast under the name "Passiontech Podcast". So I decided to share it with my near and dear ones. I got some mixed responses;

some said it was nice and one of the feedback that hit me most was that I should work on my English before I post.

I said, “Yes, I should brush up on my English and I will.

But why stop creating the content?”

English is just a universal language; it can be communicated in many ways.

If you can convey your message in your own way, why not?

Normally, junior engineers don't get vast subjects, especially in communication skills. They are mostly taught technical skills.

Junior engineers are not experts like Oxford university students because their exposure is limited!

The question is, how many Oxford students run their own content, podcasts and spread good awareness? I feel English is just a medium to share your thoughts, and it's a common communication bridge.

If you can convey your message meaningfully, English is just a means that's it. You must only know how to pass awareness.

And my mentor says, “Build a castle of your own with the bricks that were thrown at you.”

So my message to all the freshers, under-graduates, junior engineers, who just started careers and who are now facing one or the other problem concerning communication skills, there is always room to improve. But it does not mean you cannot communicate in this world, so, go-ahead.

Follow your passion

- Write a book
- Run your podcast
- Create content
- Make videos

In one week, I completed 3 podcasts and become a guest for 3 more podcasts.

- Let me Tell "U" Episode #1 How to overcome fear and live your Passion
- Let me Tell "U" Episode #2 How to be Vibrant and be Yourself
- Let me Tell "U" Episode #3 How to be Dreamer and be you in career

This list will go on and on.

"If you know the way and how to run anything, still you can win anything, language is not a barrier."

— Akhilesh Telkar

2.4.2 Importance of Passion

It's important to find the right passion. Despite the universal fantasies of winning the lottery, buying expensive cars and homes, and doing fascinating work with interesting people in exotic places, the sober reality is that most of us have to work hard for a long time. If you spend forty to fifty years—not an unlikely scenario—working at jobs you would rather not be doing, you are in truth throwing away a large part of your life. This is unnecessary and sad, especially as a career you can love is within your reach.

What Is the Ideal Career, anyway?

Passion enhances your life. It is personally fulfilling because it nourishes the most important aspects of your personality. It suits the way you like to do things and reflects who you are. It lets you use your innate strengths in ways that come naturally to you, and it doesn't force you to do things you don't do well (at least, not often).

How can you tell if you are in the right career? Here are some general guidelines. If you are not employed, keep them in mind as you search for your ideal career. If you are employed, see how your present job measures up.

Career now in the digital world, it's all about creating your value and place in the market for yourself.

"Anything That Is Closer To
Your Heart Can Win Any Movement
Anything That Is Coming From
Your Mind Can Lead You To Success."

— Akhilesh Telkar

2.4.3 21st Century Skills you can target

- Digital Marketing
- Business Development/Productivity/Systems Experts
- Sales (Funnels/advertising/High ticket Close)
- Marketing (Email/Chatbots/Growth hacking)
- Leadership
- Data Analysis/Cloud management

- Writing/Storytelling
- Brand Video Creation/Production/Podcast
- Finance Budgeting
- Customer Service/IT/Networking
- Coder/Software Development/Tester
- Artificial Intelligence/ Voice/Future Tech Development
- Social Media (Copywriting/Content/Strategy)
- Health/Mindset/Habits/Time Management
- Public Speaking/Coaching/Mentoring/Training

2.4.4 Career mantras you can consider to adopt

1. Prioritize 60 minutes of your day-to-day to read, write and memorize.
2. Set 2-3 hours a day doing focused work, and turn off notifications or any distractions when you into it (3rd Best Time – 11 am to 2 pm, 2nd Best time – 9 pm to 11 pm, 1st Best time- 5 am – 7 am).
3. Take 100% responsibility for your life without blaming circumstances or anyone.
4. Do push-ups, squats or Surya Namaskar. You can start with 5 cycles a day as a beginner, and slowly increase it to 11 cycles per day.
5. Go for healthy food- avoid high-sugar and junk food.
6. Walk along to clear the brain fog - 30 minutes preferred in the morning.
7. Spare your Sundays - spend time with family and friends.

8. Keep distance from people who only prioritize their needs over yours, they are your greatest setbacks.
9. Some people are an investment and some are bills - read this line again.
10. Quit Smoking, Quit Drugs - if you quit your bad habits, it will boost your focus and memory.
11. Spend at least 20 minutes sun-bathing without a phone.
12. Take a lighter dinner and walk at least 60-80 steps before going to bed to have better sleep.
13. Talk to high-value people – Socialize.
14. Learn a new skill and spend another 90 days developing it - you will start making money even in sleep.

CHAPTER 3

PAISA

3.1 PAISA POWER

Who Doesn't want Vitamin M? – Read paisa power subdivided into Energy, Health, Mind, Spiritual and Financial -Powers to illustrate your desire and success:

3.1.1 Energy Power

3.2.1 Health Power

3.3.1 Mind Power

3.4.1 Spiritual Power

3.5.1 financial Power

I have another interesting story to share with you. Gururaj was planning to get married and looking for a career change. He was doing very well with respect to his position in the job. However, the missing elements were money and the right partner who could support him. When he started his search for a life partner at the age of 29, he faced some challenges. The girls' parents would ask Gururaj about his salary, savings, and if he owned a house or site. Such questions bothered him.

Desperate to make money, he was under societal pressure but neither he was able to make more money, nor find the right partner for himself. As days went by, he started feeling he would not be able to make it, as once he crossed the age of 30, he would have limited options.

Then one day, he bought a ring embedded with a blue sapphire diamond. The day he started wearing it, suddenly everything started to change in his life. All that he was yearning for started happening; he got married to the girl he liked for a long time and started making money.

You may be wondering from where did Gururaj get that blue sapphire diamond ring and, how to get that one? Right?

Visit this link to order:
www.orderbluesappireluckydimond.com

Is the link working?

No?

Check again.

Is it spelled correctly?

Yes, now?

Still some error?

Oh, ok!

No? Ah, read the book till the end to get the correct answer!

The Vitamin M- Who doesn't want it?

According to the WEALTH PRINCIPLE of "Secrets of the Millionaire Mind" by T Harv Eker:

Your income can grow only to the extent you do! the money blueprint which you draw for yourself.

Why Is Your Money Blueprint Important?

Have you heard of people who have "blown up" financially? Have you noticed how some people have a lot of money and then lose it, or have excellent opportunities that start well but then go sour on them? Now you know the real cause. On the outside, it looks like bad luck, a downturn in the economy, a lousy partner, whatever. On the inside, however, it's another matter. That's why, if you come into big money when you're not ready for it on the inside, the chances are your wealth will be short-lived and you will lose it.

The vast majority of people simply do not have the internal capacity to create and hold on to large amounts of money and the increased challenges that go with more money and success.

A perfect example is lottery winners. Research has shown again and again that regardless of the size of their winnings, most lottery winners eventually return to their original financial state, the amount they can comfortably handle.

On the other hand, the opposite occurs for self-made millionaires. Notice that when self-made millionaires lose their money, they usually have it back within a relatively short time. Donald Trump and Bill Gates are good examples. Trump was worth billions, lost everything, and then, a couple of years later, got it all back again and more.

Why does this phenomenon occur? Because even though some self-made millionaires may lose their money, they never lose the most important ingredient to their success: their millionaire mindset. Of course, in "Bill Gates's case, it's his "billionaire" mind. Do you realize Bill Gates could never be just a millionaire? If he had a net worth of only 1 million dollars, how do you think he would feel about his financial success? Most people would agree that he would probably feel broke, like a financial failure!

That's because Bill Gates's financial "thermostat" is set for billions, not millions. Most people's financial thermostats are set for generating thousands, not millions of dollars; some people's financial thermostats are set for generating hundreds, not even thousands; and some people's financial thermostats are set for below zero. They are freaking freezing and they don't have a clue as to why!

The reality is that most people do not reach their full potential. Most people are not successful. Research shows that 80 percent of individuals will never be financially free in the way they would like to be, and 80 percent will never claim to be truly happy.

The reason is simple. Most people are unconscious. They are a little asleep at the wheel. They work and think on a superficial level of life—based only on what they can see. They live strictly in the visible world.

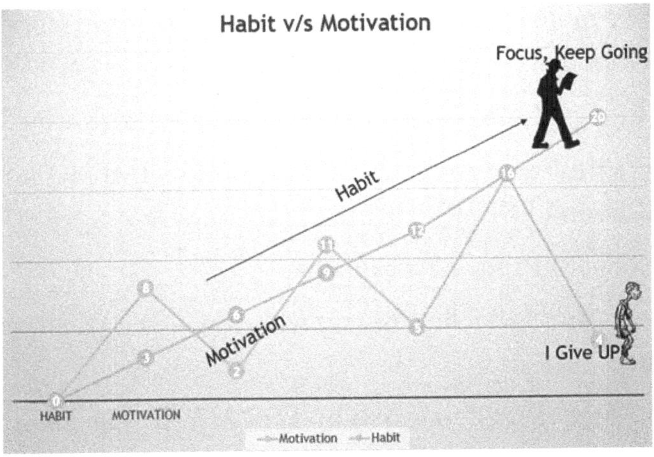

Fig 5 : Habits Vs Motivation

Secrets of the Millionaire Mind Declaration

"What I heard about money isn't necessarily true. I choose to adopt new ways of thinking that support my passion and career."

"I release my unsupportive money experiences from the past and create a new and rich future career."

"My goal is to become a millionaire and more!"

"I commit to being rich."

"I think big! I choose to help thousands and thousands of people!"

"I promote my value to others with passion and enthusiasm."

"I am an excellent receiver. I am open and willing to receive massive amounts of money into my life."

"I am an excellent money manager."

"My money works hard for me and makes me more and more money."

"I am committed to constantly learning and growing."

The Real assets in your career are your TIME, PASSION, SKILLS and EXPERIENCE.

Not your Paisa. What? Really?

Yes, Paisa will follow or stay with you only if you have the ability.

"If an Egg is broken by an outside force, Life Ends,
If broken by an inside force, Life Begins,
Great things always happen from Inside."

— Jim Kwik

You can run 100 meters in 30 seconds.

If develop your stamina through practice, you can run the same 100 meters in 20 seconds.

Those who practice for years with the help of a coach or an expert can complete in less than 12 seconds and set a world record.

What is the message here?

Successful people are no different from others, but there is one thing that sets them apart – They have decided not to do anything average. They realized early in the game that average is not going to get them anywhere. Therefore, they decided to do more than what it takes to be successful.

"TAKE MASSIVE ACTION AT 10X LEVEL".

— Grant Cardone

By this time, I started my journey toward becoming successful. I invested in various options like Mutual Funds, Post Office, Insurance, Cryptocurrency, and so on. I started thinking about how to change my financial situation.

Till today, I have both sides of this: the awareness and the gnawing drive to do more. And to be completely honest, I have never thought much about past success. I always give my attention to what is possible.

Your thoughts are both the words you hear in your head and the words you speak out loud. When you say to somebody, "What a beautiful day," you had the thought first and then spoke the words. Your thoughts also become your actions. When you get out of bed in the morning, you had the thought of getting out of bed before you took action. You can't take any action without thinking first.

It's your thoughts that determine whether your words and actions will be positive or negative. But how do you know whether your thoughts are positive or negative? Your thoughts are positive when they are thoughts of what you want and love! And negative thoughts are what you don't want and don't love. It is that simple and that easy.

Steering clear of blaming others will not improve the situation. Developing persistence is one character you want to have.

Do not pass it on to the situation or others. Work on every area of your life, regardless of the future results. Be persistent, be a doer, do your best, and the results will follow. Keep doing the work you wanted to achieve your goal. Be crazy. Nothing will happen overnight, so don't quit and don't blame.

Learn how to be strong, build your muscle, plan and see how much you can persist.

If you don't tune your frequency - Just like the right station for your favorite channel on the radio - The channel you tune up to will play. So in life - the channel, in fact, the frequency you choose to tune in will continue to be the same as you grow. If you tune in for problems, lies, cheating and corruption, the same will continue. If you tune up your frequency to complain about a situation, fear problems, blame others, regrets, hatred, cravings, etc., you start developing this frequency and your channel will tune up to the same frequency all the time. Change your frequency to positive thinking, being truthful, following the path of dharma, doing good, receiving good, and other important things. However, this will not happen unless you don't address all areas of life-like Health, Relationships, Career and Wealth.

If you want to change your current status, you have to decide and prepare your mindset–. If you do not believe that you deserve success, popularity and money, this is not going to happen for you. So, first thing in the morning, stand in front of the mirror and say you are successful, you are a money magnet; you live the happy life that you deserve.

Desire to achieve them, because if this doesn't happen in your mind in the first place, then it won't happen in reality.

History shows that morning Visualization, Affirmations and Gratitude are the keys to success for most successful personalities. Let's learn more about this in the upcoming chapter.

"Don't get struck at one level,
do more than your potential."

— Akhilesh Telkar

3.1.1 ENERGY POWER

3.1.1.1: Energy

Energy is everything

In modern society, physical power is now replaced with paper money with an assigned value, but the energy exchange is still the same. Money is simply energy. To get what we want, we trade our money (energy) for the value (energy) of something else. It is a give-and-take policy.

The Law of Attraction believes that we and our thoughts are made of pure energy and that positive energy attracts positive energy, whereas negative energy can only bring more negative energy. This theory asks you to start thinking about your life in a new way.

In essence, your energy is very valuable, it's like money. You should only invest your time and energy into the things that you admire most. The return you are looking for is that "YOU" get something out of it, whether it is money, or more energy, or personal fulfillment.

To attract success in your career, you have to vibrate at certain energy levels. If your energy vibrates at a lower level, then it does not match your success energy. You have to tune-up to match that energy level.

If you can match the energy level all the time as successful people vibrate, then you will be more successful than you are. Then success is sure.

Points to remember:

1. Albert Einstein — 'Energy cannot be created or destroyed, it can only be changed from one form to another.
2. Everything in this universe is made of Energy, the total amount of energy in this universe is constant and there is one energy in the universe.
3. Scientifically, we all have one energy. Everything in the universe is one God. All religions refer to the

same energy, that energy is within us and we vibrate at different frequencies. The way I look is different from the way you look because we generate different energy.

4. Energy flows where your attention goes, and so when you direct the energy of gratitude toward another person's needs, that's where the energy goes.
5. If I change my energy level, I can change my life.

Learn more about the same at https://akhileshtelkar.co.in/

3.2.1 : HEALTH POWER

3.2.1.1 Health is Wealth

One day, I was telling an old friend that we wouldn't live beyond 60 years. He agreed, and many others thought the same way, because the foods we eat, the habits we have, and the climate we live in are not so conducive to a long life.

By reading many books and following some great spirituals, I realized we can live up to 100 years if we build healthy habits.

The world is going back to its roots like Yoga, Meditation, and spiritual power are emerging back.

3.2.2.1 Being Fit or Being Aware!!!

From the day I heard about 'Being FIT', my mind started wandering, trying to ask myself how to be FIT and what I have to do to remain- Fit...

Then I started writing this...

1. Being Healthy : Follow Diets, Eat healthy and Exercise
2. Going behind : Work out, Challenge your limits and Run the extra mile

What do you think of the above two?

In my opinion, there is a 3rd option as well, it may be right or wrong, it's just my understanding...

3. Being Aware : Being Fit means Being Aware of your daily habits, focusing...

What is the one thing you do daily:

without fail,

without missing,

without forgetting,

with interest,

with love,

with hungry

What if you have to choose between Healthy (being Aware) V/S Unhealthy (Losing focus)?

Being Aware means:

Eat - 3/4 of your capacity

Avoid - Junk Food

After Eating - Walking a minimum of 60 steps

You can use a staircase and indulge yourself in physical activities.

What if such activities make you aware of your actions and help you focus on being #Fit? Won't that be great?

Start helping yourself - Like switching on the light/fan for yourself, getting up to pick that water bottle, if you forgot your bike/car keys- going back inside to fetch them, etc. Being aware of fitness is self-help.

What's your opinion?

Share your opinion *#finduinyou@akhileshtelkar*

To have a great life in the coming years, you have to set up a proper daily routine; it is all about health.

Choose your days wisely

- If Days are good, Months become productive,
- If Months are wise enough, Automatically Years become wise,
- If your Years are wise, then Life becomes way beyond wonderful than you think.

So how can you reach that health level and be energetic the whole day?

1. Before going to bed, keep a journal, and write the accomplishments you like to achieve.
2. The moment you wake up, thank the universe. Read/ write your accomplishments.

3. Start your day with affirmations and gratitude.
4. Do not forget to address all areas of life: Health, Wealth, Relationship Career.
5. Writing them on a daily basis is very important.
6. To keep your mind active and functioning at great levels, give your mind some peace by meditating. The secret mantra of many successful people is they start their day with meditation, yoga and some light exercises.
7. It is necessary to build and maintain your energy level. For this, you must do exercise, walk or run, depending upon your health routine.
8. I call it transformation mornings, which I do every day early morning. This must be a part of your daily routine. Join me at -https://akhileshtelkar.co.in/

Quit Blaming: Stop blaming yourself for not achieving anything so far, quit blaming your parents, situation, career, teachers, marriage, kids and so on.

Before you manifest consciously, you attain what you want. So, live a purposeful life and use your time effectively.

ACTIVITY 16

Keep one hand on your heart, the other on your mind and say:

"I am ready to be disciplined"

"I am ready to succeed in "Passion, Career & Paisa"

"I am ready to use my time effectively"

Use your time effectively by breaking important goals/ tasks into smaller chunks:

1. Divide your 24 hours by 2, one half is Productive hours and the second Non-Productive hours.
2. Take out your productive hours and divide them into smaller chunks, let's say, 12/4 =3 hours per task.
3. Now select which is the most important goal/ task.
4. Dedicate the first 3 hours completely to that important task every day and work until it gets complete.
5. Keep a target date to complete.
6. Declare your goal to your loved ones. Either they will discourage you or encourage you to do (both will benefit).

3.2.2.2 : Bonus Health Tips

— Eat the fruit that has been touched by a worm.

— Boldly pick the mushroom on which the insects sit.

— Plant the tree where the mole digs.

— Go to sleep and wake up at the same time as the birds – you will reap all the day's golden grains.

— Eat more greens: you will have strong legs and a resistant heart, like the beings of the forest.

— Swim often and you will feel on earth like the fish in the water.

— Look at the sky as often as possible and your thoughts will become light and clear.

— Be quiet a lot, speak little – and silence will come in your heart, and your spirit will be calm and full of peace.

— *Saint Seraphim of Sarov*

3.2.3 : BILLIONAIRES MANTRAS! (~ RAFAEL BADZIAG)

1. **Early to Bed and Early to Rise Makes a Man Healthy Wealthy Wise**

   Studies reveal that every single billionaire waking up early is a big driver of their success. Most wealthy people wake up between 4:30 am to 5:30 am.

   Morning hours.

   Sun Rise Time – Primary Energy is good for Health.

   The Silence – Observe the silence, it increases thinking capacity.

   No Noise – Fresh Air, no disturbance allows you to feel fresh

   Undisturbed time – Helps you to increase productivity and mentally prepare for the day.

   Ahead of Time – Starting early keeps you ahead of others when others are still asleep.

   It's important to note that getting less sleep isn't what makes you successful. There are very few billionaires who only need between three to four hours of sleep, but the majority of them function best after seven to eight hours of rest. Those that need more sleep simply go to bed earlier.

2. **They keep healthy**

   No Health ⟶ No Wealth ⟶ No Wealth ⟶ No Happiness ⟶ No Happiness ⟶ What's the point in Living!

   Irrespective of your age – Commit to this, make a habit to your routine Exercise ⟶ Meditate ⟶ Yoga, etc.

   Whether they are in mid-age or above 60, all billionaires maintain their health by exercising regularly.

   It was interesting to learn that many billionaires incorporate their favorite sports into their workout regimen. They claim that sports teach you about winning and losing, both of which are essential skills in business and life.

   Sports aren't the only element of a healthy life for billionaires. Many practice meditation or stick to a nutritious diet. Most billionaires either are non-smokers or drop unhealthy habits.

3. **They read**

   Warren Buffett, a great reader, shares that reading is the most valuable source of knowledge. Bill Gates reads 50-60 books a year.

   Many billionaires just read the economy pages of national dailies. Many prefer the likes of The Economist, Financial Times, Daily News, etc.

   Others go for biographies of iconic business leaders or books about sports, finance, business, science, history or technology. They also learn a lot from fiction and self-help books.

Young people should read. Read books about how to do things right. Read books about how to build a great mindset and character.

It helps to develop a systematic approach to your reading: Keep a priority list of titles based on your interests or recommendations from mentors — anything that will add value to your life. If you want to go the extra mile, mark interesting passages and write down notes, thoughts and ideas.

4. **Spend Me-Time**

   Billionaires love setting aside alone time...to think. They might do this by meditating, sitting in silence, going for a walk in the moonlight or on the beach or some other relaxing activity they enjoy.

   Media mogul Oprah Winfrey is a strong advocate for meditation.

They commit to routines

Routines and rituals are sets of habits that, when practiced consistently, lead to profound, long-term results. Most billionaire routines start early in the day.

It doesn't matter when you do your routine activities. What counts is that you commit to doing them — even when you don't feel like it.

Some have simpler routines, some more complex ones, but as I mentioned earlier, typical elements of a billionaire morning routine include getting up early, exercising, reading and contemplating.

5. **They practice discipline**

   Billionaires are some of the most disciplined people. They set extraordinarily high standards for themselves and the people around them.

   In sports, for example, you can't achieve great results if you don't have enough discipline to train regularly. The same applies to your life and career. Limit the distractions and temptations that hinder your progress. Show up. Be eager to grow your skills.

   Of course, billionaires are by no means superhumans. Like the rest of us, they have days where they feel lazy and unmotivated. The difference, however, is that they are fully aware of it and don't allow themselves to slack off. They get power through their struggles.

   Limit the distractions and temptations that hinder your progress. Show up. Be eager to grow your skills.

   Learn more about the same in - https://akhileshtelkar.co.in/

The Make-Up Mornings

1. M - Majestic Gratitude
2. A - Affirmation
3. K - Knowledge
4. E - Exercise
5. U- Urge
6. P- Prayers

3.3 MIND POWER

3.3.1: Law of Universe (Gratitude and Thank you)

Why say thank you?

In our childhood, our parents and elders taught us to say thank you in return for favors or things we received, agree?

But the truth is as we grow along, it just becomes a habit. But we never notice the actual power of it. In reality, we didn't realize how many miracles and wonders the word "thank you" can create.

One truth everyone agrees in all the world is that being grateful helps, but nobody makes us understand why we should be thankful and what happens when someone ignores this.

Introducing one more term "Universe" - whether you call it God, you believe in your religion, you follow your rituals, at the end of every act you do, everything counts and you send these energies to the Universe.

Knowingly or unknowingly, you become part of a good or bad act where the universe registers your act.

Expressing gratitude to the Universe for everything you have unfolds your true potential and you will receive more happiness and abundance in return.

As per Rhonda Byrne, the author of "The Magic":

No matter who you are, no matter where you are and no matter your current circumstances, being grateful and thankful will open up new rays of hope to you.

- Those who aren't thankful to the universe for whatever

they have, will never find it.

- It's as real as you are. In fact, life can be far more wondrous than you ever thought it was as a child, and more breathtaking, awe-inspiring, and exciting than anything you have seen before.
- Are you ready to experience the miracles again? Are you ready to be filled with awe and wonder every day, like when you were a child? Get ready for the Miracles.
- Whoever is more grateful to the universe, whoever is more thankful to the universe will be given more, and he will have an abundance. Whoever does not, even what he has, will be taken away from him.

The hidden truth behind success stories that has eluded many for centuries is in being Grateful.

It works on the fundamental law of science and of the Universe.

What if you have the chance to go back to your childhood, will you be happy to go or not? Remember those days, how life was magical and exciting. Even the smallest things were utterly thrilling. We used to be in our own world. It gave us immense joy to try new things without thinking too much. We were fascinated by small drops of water on grass/leaf, the colors of butterflies, the rainbow, the strange look of trees, the shape of the clouds and many more.

We used to get excited about the festivals:

Ganesh Chaturthi : Placing Ganesh idols in places like empty fields/on roads/areas.

Sankranthi : Wearing a new dress and distributing Ellu/Bella to all our near and dear ones.

Holi : The festival of colors that we celebrated with family and friends, mass gatherings and having fun on the streets.

Deepawali : Known as the 'festival of lights', we celebrate Diwali by lighting lamps and bursting crackers.

Ramadan : Fasting, prayers and biriyani.

Christmas : Even though we had no idea how Santa could come to every child in the world in one night, somehow, he did through our actors and never let us down.

Our hearts would be full of joy, our imagination had no limits, and we believed that life is magical.

Every day was a new day, full of promises, more excitement and adventure.

However, as we grew into adults, when we start getting into our responsibilities, our nature started to shift towards reality and we became one of them all.

The problems and difficulties took over us, and our childhood days started to fade away.

This is the reason I asked earlier: How about if you get a chance to go back to your childhood days?

Even if it is for some moments, most of us would say YES!

Life can be far more wonderful than you ever thought.

Read further....

According to Rhonda Byrne- Be Grateful and express thanks to the universe for your entire life. According to the law of attraction, which governs all the energy in our

Universe, from the formation of an atom to the movement of the planets, "like attracts like". It's because of the law of attraction that the cells of every living creature are held together, as well as the substance of every material object. In your life, the law operates on your thoughts and feelings, because they are energy too, and so whatever you think, whatever you feel, you attract to you.

"Whatever goes around comes around," "You reap what you sow," and "You get what you give."

Buddha said that you have no cause for anything but gratitude and joy.

"When you arise in the morning, give thanks for the morning light, for your life and strength. Give thanks for your food and the joy of living."

— Tecumseh

History is laden with famous figures who practiced gratitude, and whose achievements put them among the greatest human beings who have ever lived: Gandhi, Mother Teresa, the Dalai Lama, Shakespeare, Abraham Lincoln, Isaac Newton, Albert Einstein, and many, many more.

The scientists, philosophers, inventors, discoverers, and prophets who practiced gratitude reaped its results, and most were aware of its inherent power. Yet still, gratitude's power is unknown to most people today because to experience the magic of gratitude in life you have to practice it!

Gratitude can magically turn your relationships into joyful and meaningful relationships, no matter what state they are in now. Gratitude can miraculously make you more prosperous so that you have the money you need to do the things you want to do. It will increase your health and bring a level of happiness beyond what you've ever felt before. Gratitude will work its magic to accelerate your career, increase success, and bring about your dream job or whatever it is you want to do. In fact, whatever it is that you want to be, do, or have, gratitude is the way to receive it. The magical power of gratitude turns your life into gold!

You can tell right now how much gratitude you have expressed in your life. Just take a look at all the major areas in your life: money, health, happiness, career, home, and relationships.

3.3.2 The Magic Formula: Gratitude

Deliberately think and say the magic words, thank you.

The more you deliberately think and say the magic words, thank you, the more gratitude you feel.

The more gratitude you deliberately think and feel, the more abundance you receive.

Sit down with a computer or pen and paper and make a list of what you want in every area of your life. Think through every detail of what you want to be, do, or have in your life – in your relationships, career, finances, health, and in every area that is important to you. You can be as specific and detailed as you like, but remember, your job is simply to list what you want, not how you are going to get what you want. The "how" will be done for you when gratitude starts working its magic.

ACTIVITY 17

Place one hand on your heart, the other on your mind and say:

"I am Grateful"

"I am thankful to find Passion, Career & Paisa"

"I am thankful for this beautiful life"

Gratitude examples:

I am grateful for everything I have. Thank you, thank you, thank you!

I am grateful for my journey and path. Thank you, thank you, thank you!

I am grateful to mother earth. Thank you, thank you, thank you!

I am grateful for the new day, thank you that I woke up early. Thank you, thank you, thank you!

I am grateful to my parents, caretakers; thank you, thank you, thank you!

I am grateful I am healthy, thank you for my body, face, hands, legs, and everything I got from the universe. Thank you, thank you, thank you!

I am grateful to the universe that I am blessed with a healthy family. Thank you, thank you, thank you!

I am grateful to the people who supported me. Thank you, thank you, thank you!

I am grateful for my career. Thank you, thank you, thank you!

I am grateful for all the money I have. Thank you, thank you, thank you!

"Gratitude operates through a universal law that governs whole life."

Affirmations:

Today is my day. Today, I will see, feel and do Something Good. Today is going to be the happiest day, Enjoyable Day, New Day, New Hope and a New Day to Find "U" in "YOU".

I am the Best

I am Smart

I am Creative

I am a Problem-Solution Expert

I am a Winner

I am a Leader

I am a Millionaire

I am a Legend

I am a Career-Passion Builder

I Love what I do

My Good Actions are Fruitful

Through the Days and Nights, I am Prospering by all means

"Whoever has gratitude (for money) will be given more, and she or he will have an abundance. Whoever does not have gratitude (for money), even what she or he has will be taken from her or him.

Sit down and take a few minutes to think back through your childhood before you had any or much money. As you recall each memory where money was paid for you, say and feel the magic words, thank you.

All of these things cost Value, and you received them all – at no charge! As you travel back through memories of your childhood and youth, you'll realize how many things you received that equate to hard-earned money. Be grateful for every single instance and memory, because when you can feel sincere gratitude for the money you've received in the past, your money will magically increase in the future! It is guaranteed by Universal law."

— Rhonda Byrne

Learn more about this at - https://akhileshtelkar.co.in/

3.3.3 Subconscious Mind - Most powerful tool

A word of wisdom: Saving for a rainy day might sound like a good idea, but it can create big problems. If you are saving your money for a rainy day, what are you going to get? Rainy days! Stop doing that. Instead of saving for a rainy day, focus on saving for a joyous day or for the day you win your financial freedom. Then, by virtue of the law of intention, that's exactly what you will get.

The reason or motivation you have for making money or creating success is vital. If your motivation for acquiring money or success comes from a non-supportive root, such as fear, anger, or the need to "prove" yourself, your money will never bring you happiness.

"If You Add Suffering, Complaints and Regrets to Your Mind - Your Imagination Goes Bad. Instead, Fill it with Creativity, Love, Compassion and Forgiveness."

— T Harv Eker

"If you look around, why one person is unhappy, and another happy to the filth? Why one person is successful and another person is poor and miserable? Why is one person fearful, whereas another is full of faith and confidence? Why does one person have a luxurious home while another man lives in a hut? Why is one person an outstanding and popular speaker, and another craving to get established? Why is one person a genius in his work or profession while the other man struggles throughout his life without accomplishing anything? Why is one person suffering from an incurable disease and another isn't? Why do so many good, kind and religious people suffer and another person prospers and enjoys radiant health? Why is one woman happily married and her sister or friend very frustrated? Is there an answer to these questions? In the workings of your conscious and subconscious minds, there most certainly is."

— Dr. Joseph Murphy

Let me ask you another question.

Which is the most powerful weapon in this whole world?

Think! Think! Think!

The answer is our Mind! It has an infinite treasure inside it, the more you dig, the more value you get. Believe me. If you open your mental eyes, learn to unfold and behold treasure within you, you can live gloriously, abundantly and happily.

Many are unaware of this gold mine hidden inside. They are asleep and don't know how to use it. Whatever you want, you can draw from it.

You can bring into your life more power, more health, more wealth, more happiness, and more joy by learning to utilize the hidden power of your subconscious mind.

We live in two states of mind:

1. *Conscious Mind:* Represents your body, environment and all your affairs.
2. *Subconscious Mind:* It takes orders you give it based upon what your conscious mind believes and accepts as true.

Conscious Mind: What we feel, what we see, and what we are aware of happening.

Subconscious Mind: Something always awake even when we sleep. It works for 24 hours and never rests. Our subconscious registers whatever the conscious mind accepts. It gets fed into the subconscious mind. This mind does not know whether the information is true or false. It believes as it is.

It works all the time and takes signals.

Let me give examples of what I learned and how I used it.

According to Joseph Murphy, "*Think good - Good follows, Think Evil - Evil follows.*"

The subconscious mind has the power of making your muscles strong. It sends signals to different levels, heals others and you as well.

Warning: Keep in mind that it works effectively when you use this with good intentions.

The best examples are all available in and around.

As you say, I cannot do it, and repeatedly tell your subconscious mind that you can't do it, then the result turns out to be that you can't.

Example 1: When you return home from the day's of office work, you say that you are tired. Your elders or parents hear it, and they start telling you that you look very tired, take rest, take some energy drinks, or don't do anything, sit or lean. After hearing these words, you feel even more tired.

It adds up to your subconscious mind, you won't feel like doing anything and you start to feel tired and sleepy.

Example 2: You want to buy a house or a car or dream job- and say repeatedly that it is not meant for me, it's costly and I can't afford this. As long as you keep saying this to yourself, definitely you won't get it.

If you see in a few cases mentioned below, they silently wished for things to happen and it happened with them:

1. It's funny but remember in (DDLJ), Shahrukh says to himself "Palat, Palat, Palat" on the 3rd time, Kajol turns. How does this happen?

   It transpires only when two people want it to happen. They can connect or feel even from a distance. (I tried this in school days, and it worked for me. I was surprised after knowing this. Are you?)

2. Another best example is - Two people are deeply connected, it happens that they utter the same words and at the same time.
3. We normally hear that some friends are chitchatting and suddenly the person whom they are remembering turns up. The friends say that we have been talking about you and you have shown up.
4. You might have heard people saying, 'When we started constructing our house, we never thought it was possible, we have done it with God's grace.
5. I always wanted to buy this car -finally, the day has come.
6. I never thought I would crack this interview- lucky to get my dream company.
7. I never thought I could start a business- I did it with all intentions.

So, maybe you do some silent prayers, bring positive energy, deliberately remember that person, start saying yes, I can, I have plans to buy it, I can manage this, I will buy it. Automatically, your subconscious mind starts getting positive signals. You send the right signals, and things start to work.

My mentor advised me to read the book "The Power of Subconscious Mind " by Joseph Murphy. I was amazed by the kind of results he has explained in the book.

The week I complete this book, my mom got a health issue. She had been facing that problem for quite a long time, but this time the doctor suggested going for major surgery D&C Biopsy later Hysterectomy (a surgical procedure to remove the womb (uterus)).

Mom was very healthy, and always maintained a good diet, but the only problem I saw with mom was that she got influenced by negative words. She heard about an illness; she would think that small illnesses can create big problems.

I did not know that affirming positive things would be of such great help.

I use mom's weakness as a tool.

The only thing I told mom was, "The doctors want to heal your problems permanently, so they will do a minor operation on you. They have said that after this operation, you will feel much healthier than before."

Mom believed that she would be much healthier after this operation. Now, it was in her subconscious mind the operation was for her betterment.

Here's one more thing I told mom to keep in mind:

Start imagining and tell yourself that because the doctor has identified your health issue, now you are much healthier than before.

As per the Subconscious mind, we can heal others by Affirming.

I also told my family members and everyone to say the same.

I applied this technique for one week continuously.

I said this day and night to my subconscious mind "My mom is much healthier than before. She does not have any more health issues."

After one week, the doctor asked us to go for an ultrasound of the abdomen and pelvis. When they did the ultrasound - the gynecologist was shocked. She said that the formation of the endometrium had thickened and become heterogeneous. It measured 21.7mm and showed cystic changes. The lab doctor said that we should have come and shown it to the doctor before.

My mom got a little worried. But still, we had to take the advice from the main doctor. She made two suggestions:

1. Biopsy - one-day admission
2. Decision about the major surgery after the next report

So, we had to decide at home and plan the date for the operation.

Everyone was worried, but I maintained the same belief that it was a minor operation and after this, everything will be fine.

I got mom admitted, and it was time for the test. The doctor spent a day at the hospital for the whole procedure. She and his staff were kind enough to give mom proper care.

Mom was in the OT inside, and I was sitting outside, praying silently.

I directed my subconscious mind to think positively. I imagined that everything had gone well and mom was feeling healthy and better than before.

After some time, the doctor called me to tell me about the report.

To the doctor's surprise, there is no infection in the uterus. They took the samples and sent those to the lab.

Now I had to wait for that report to decide on the major surgery.

The report came after 5 days.

All our prayers worked, in fact, the subconscious mind sent the right signals to the universe!

Guess what? My mom did not require major surgery.

She was fine. Only a few tablets were good enough to heal further.

So, I wonder how this was possible. Is it a miracle or science? However, do not think much.

Believe in the power of the subconscious mind, but you should not neglect medical emergencies. Both are equally important.

Use your subconscious mind in the right way: Try this for the benefit of others and your career.

Your subconscious mind is the book of your life. Whatever thoughts, beliefs, opinions or theories you write for yourself inside, you will experience it outside.

"Man is what he thinks all the day long."

— Ralph Waldo Emerson

Things to remember:

1. Your subconscious mind controls all the vital processes of your body - input positive to receive positive results.
2. Every night prior to sleep - send a specific request to the subconscious mind about the problems to solve or things you like to pursue for the next day - see the miracles working.
3. Whatever you impress on your subconscious mind is expressed on the screen of space as conditions, experiences and events. Therefore, you should carefully watch all ideas and thoughts entertained in your conscious mind.
4. The law of action and reaction is universal. Your thought is action, and the reaction is the automatic response of your subconscious mind to your thought. Watch your thoughts!

Again, your subconscious conditioning determines your thinking. Your thinking determines your decisions, and your decisions determine your actions, which eventually determine your outcomes.

"Whatever the mind can conceive and believe, it can achieve."

— Napoleon Hill,

Think and Grow Rich

ACTIVITY 18

AWARENESS: Write down all the statements you have heard about money, wealth, and rich people when you were young.

UNDERSTANDING: Write down how you believe these statements have affected your financial life so far.

DECLARATION: Place one hand on your heart, the other on your mind and say:

"I am ready to become aware"

"I am ready to find Passion, Career & Paisa"

"I am ready to become a money magnet"

"What I heard about money isn't necessarily true. I choose to adopt new ways of thinking that support my happiness and success."

— T Harv Eker

Learn more about this at: https://akhileshtelkar.co.in/

3.4 SPIRITUAL POWER

3.4.1 Vipasanna

After completing ten days, of course, I arrived back home.

It was 10:21 am and my niece (Avani; name changed) was standing at the entrance gate.

The moment she saw me, she gestured to me with a happy voice (because she had come to my home when I wasn't there).

Avani: Hi maama!

Me: Hey, there!

Avani: Where have you been for the last ten days?

Me: I have been to "Vipassana".

Avani: Vipassana? What's that?

Me: It's a meditation center.

Avani: Why did you go there?

Me: For mind service, haha.

Avani: Does the mind also need service?

Me: Yes, of course, why not?

Airplanes, automobiles, and any equipment, anything which is movable or mechanical, non-moveable electrical and electronics which are created by man need service, agree?

Avani: Yup.

Me: Our mind projects 6.5 thoughts per minute and 60000+ thoughts per day.

Avani: Omg.

Me: Yeah, Google it if you don't believe.

Avani: Hmmm.

Me: So, we need to calm down and take care of this tiny little intelligent part of the human body and give some peace to our mind. In short, we need regular service to enhance its performance. Do you know which is the best place to service your mind?

Avani: I don't know.

Me: Meditation is the best suggestion for mind matters, and the best place to service your mind is Vipassana.

Avani: I am excited to know more about Vipassana.

Me: It's an ancient technique taught by Gautama Buddha. After years of research, he found a straightforward approach based on the law of nature, which would help humankind. It's Buddha's greatest gift to all.

Avani: Oh, interesting.

Me: Vipassanā (Pāli) or vipaśyanā (Sanskrit), literally "special, super (Vi), seeing (Passanā)," is a Buddhist term that is often translated as "insight." The essence of teaching by Buddha is a miracle that was discovered 2500 years ago, the experience of truth in which he spoke about the art of living. Buddha did not teach any religion or philosophy or system of belief. He called his teaching Dhamma "law", the law of nature. He offered a universal practical solution for a universal problem.

Vipassana is a great technique and a unique methodology, and it is still in practice because of its simplicity.

Avani: Okay, how one can learn about this?

Me: Vipassana is open to anyone. It is taught by Padma Shree awarded Mr. S.N. Goenka Ji, and it has many centers in India. One can apply online for ten days, three days, or even a one-day course.

Avani: Anyone?

Me: Ya, if one sincerely wishes to learn the technique and is willing to do so physically and mentally.

The best part is that it is free of charge, and there are other facilities like food, stay, and valuable teachings.

Avani: Why it is required to do so?

Me: The process of Vipassana has worked in the past, and it is a technique by Gautam Aditya Buddha. He found it within himself when the changes happened, and when he felt enlightened, he started teaching this beautiful technique to others.

The changes persist even after they occur. Whatever mental strength was given in the system can be applied in daily life to benefit the good of others. Life becomes more harmonious, fruitful, and happy.

Avani: Great. How are you feeling after completing now?

Me: Before going to the Vipassana, I posted on FB/LinkedIn about the servicing of the mind. Still, after attending the course, one must agree that teachers say this is no ordinary service. It's the deepest of most profound mind service.

Before going to the Vipassana was unaware of meditation; I wanted to find myself and write my book.

Find ”U” in “You”; the only way to experience truth directly is to look within to observe oneself, so I decided to take up this course.

In addition to Vipassana, I have an interesting story to share.

Once a man was lost in the desert, unable to find his way back home; he had lost food, water, and everything. He only found sand and empty land wherever he saw. So he started walking for several kilometers and hours.

He could not reach his place because he was unsure if he was headed down the correct path. With no choice, he started walking in a direction, fearing that he might get exhausted and die there. He saw a water pump at a distance; he gathered all his energy to walk towards the water pump. He let out a sigh of relief because only water could save him from dying. The man was very thirsty and winds of sand splashed over his face. The sand was going in his mouth, and he was desperately looking for water. As he started pumping, he noticed there was no water. He pumped twice and checked again, but no sign of water. He pumped for 3 to 4 more times but no water. This continued for some time. He pumped but not even a drop of water surfaced.

The man was disappointed and had lost all his energy. So, he decided to move on, but before leaving, he pumped the water pump very hard with full strength one last time. After he walked a few steps, he turned around and noticed there was one drop of water from the inlet. He ran and sucked that drop. Happy to have tasted that one drop of water on his tongue, he felt great and decided to pump hard enough to get some more water. He poured in his entire strength and, little by little, water started dripping. He drank happily until his stomach was full. Then he splashed water on his face, his head, and then his entire body. He felt pleased that he had finally got water. Whatever he had, like a bottle, cover, etc., he filled it so that he could carry a little further on his journey and decided to move on...

Then he suddenly stumbled on a small stone, which makes him recall his instinct. He picked up that stone, returned to the pump, and then wrote on the pump in the big letter "**it works**"...

So what is the lesson from the story?

Sometimes, in life, we lose our focus in finding the answers:

1. Which path to go?
2. Where to go?
3. What next to do?
4. Whom to contact?

Because what you consume every day, today, every time matters the most. If you want to become the person you admire the most, stop looking for answers on the outside and start answering the questions that come from the inside.

I struggled in my career and even when I decided to write this book. I gained more clarity, more wisdom, more power to handle any situation in life when I found the formula for "Find "U" in "You" by following my passion. My biggest realization is that I am mixing my Passion and technical skill = Passiontech.

Find "U" in You" is a movement to me; join me in spreading goodness; let's spread the magic of love.

Just like the desert man's story where he writes "it works" on the pump and makes a path for others, let's create a desire for a better life…

Note: The Dhamma (Dharma) path must be followed, and the teaching must be implemented; otherwise, it is a meaningless exercise.

"Don't stop when you are tired. Stop when you are done."

— David Goggins

3.4.2 Prayers & Silva technique

In India, temples are considered the highest spiritual place for prayers.

One day, as usual, a poojari opens the temple door early in the morning and starts his rituals.

One little girl, neatly dressed in a traditional dress, comes to the temple and stands before the idol. Closing her eyes with folded hands, she murmurs something for a couple of minutes, bows down, smiles and goes out running. The poojari watches closely and smiles.

The next morning again, the little girl does the same and runs away. This becomes her daily affair.

7 days passed and the poojari now couldn't resist but to find out more about her behavior.

One morning, he reaches there before the girl and waits for her to complete her ritual. He places his hand on the girl's head and says, "My child, I have been seeing since the last 7 days that you come here regularly. What do you do?"

"I pray," she says spontaneously. "Do you know any prayers?" asks the Poojari with some suspicion in his voice. "No," replies the girl. "Then what do you do after closing your eyes, every day?" he smiles.

Very innocently the girl answers, "I do not know any prayer, but I know a, b, c, d.... up to z. I recite it five times and tell God that I don't know your prayer, but it cannot be outside of these alphabets.

Please arrange these alphabets as you wish and that is my prayer." And she runs and jumps on her way out.

The poojari stands there dumbstruck, staring at her for a long time as she disappears, running into the wilderness.

This is THE UNCONDITIONAL belief in God that we pray.

Faith in the 'divine power' that heals the mind and body...

The Silva Method is a self-help and meditation program developed by José Silva. It claims to increase an individual's abilities through relaxation, the development of higher brain functions.

Technique

The technique aims to reach and sustain a state of mental functioning, called alpha state, where brainwave frequency is seven to fourteen Daydreaming and the transition to sleeping are alpha states.

Silva claimed to have developed a program that trained people to enter certain brain states of enhanced awareness. He also claimed to have developed several systematic mental processes to use while in these states, allowing a person to mentally project with a specific intent. According to Silva, once the mind is projected, a person can allegedly view distant objects or locations and connect with higher intelligence for guidance. The information received by the projected mind is then said to be perceived as thoughts, images, feelings, smells, tastes and sounds by the mind. The information obtained in this manner can be acted upon to solve problems.

ACTIVITY 19

Place one hand on your heart, the other on your mind and say:

"I am ready to dream my growth"

"I am ready to find Passion, Career & Paisa"

"I am ready to fulfill my desire"

Using the Silva Mind Control Method for Active Goal Setting:

Step 1 : Desire. Think about what you want to accomplish.

Step 2 : Belief. This step is critical to your success.

Step 3 : Expectancy. You must expect that you will accomplish your goal.

Step 4 : Positive.

Step 5 : Visualize the Accomplished Goal.

"The greatest discovery you will ever make is the potential of your own mind."

— Jose Silva

The best things are yet to happen, it always takes time.

If you come across any mixed and unpleasant situation, here are three powerful and simple questions to ask yourself:

1. What have I learned from those experiences?
2. What can be done differently now? What difference could be made?
3. What am I going to do now?

Your financial blueprint consists of a combination of your thoughts, feelings, and actions in the arena of money.

So how is your money blueprint formed? The answer is simple. Your financial blueprint consists primarily of the information or "programming" you received in the past, especially as a young child.

Who were the primary sources of this programming or conditioning? For most people, the list includes; loved ones and caretakers.

Most of us are goalless. Before setting a goal, there are three important factors to include: Vision, Mission and Micro-niche.

Vision - Broader View of the future road map

It's a myth that vision is meant only for companies or big organizations. To grow in your career, vision is something that drives you to a long life.

How do you want to see the world around you? A stress-free world, worry-free world? What kind of world do you like to create? How do you like to live in this world?

Mission - How many and whom

Micro-niche - Narrow down to your particular area of expertise/audience

"One time work = Lifetime Success"

Career means not only your professional and personal goals, but other goals are also important.

Family Goals: Goals Which You Want To Fulfill For Your Kids, Pattens, Siblings, Cousins, How Can You Contribute To Their Life, How Can You Help Them Achieve Their Life Goals, How Can You Give Them A Blissful Life So Many Times In Running Our Own Races We Forget.

Spouse Goals: Achieve With Your Spouse's Dream, Places You Want To Go With Him/Her, Lifestyle You Want To Live With Him/Her, You Are Fulfilling His/Her Aspirations, Things Which Make Him/Her Proud Of You And Which Will Make Him/Her Understand And Believe That He/She is Truly Blessed With A Life Partner Like You.

Health Goals: You Physical Fitness, Mental Fitness, Your Food And Nutrition Goals, Your Energy Goals, Stamina, Endurance, Meditation, Immunity.

Social Goals: Goals Which You Make To Give Back To The Society, Your CSR, How Do You Want To Contribute, How Do You Want To Make The World A Better Place, What Will You Do For Others? Giving And Forgetting.

Spiritual Goals: Spiritual Goals Are Things You Want To Do, Which Will Help You To Connect With God, Make You Feel Fulfilled, Like Some Practices Example- Yoga, Meditation, Attending Discourses, Satsangs, Being Part of Spiritual Community, Raise Your Consciousness, Understanding Life, and Raising Yourself Spiritually.

The Silva technique founded by Dr. Jos Silva is a boon to humankind. Learning this technique encourages people to have higher goals and ideals in all areas of their life. The typical person who practices the Silva technique has physical health and fitness levels way above the norm, practices meditation daily, and is an enthusiast of reading, fitness and spiritual growth.

The transformation in body, mind and spirit that happens to people who do practice daily yoga, meditation, exercise is one of the unique things they live and breathe self-growth.

Your career will change your body shape, and the way you dress and carry yourself. It will increase your levels of compassion, kindness and humility and you will evolve as a human being.

ACTIVITY 20

Place one hand on your heart, the other on your mind and say:

"I am ready to have a vision"

"I am ready to find Passion, Career & Paisa"

"I am ready to Transform"

1. Write your Vision statement.

   ____

2. Write your Mission statement.

   ____

3. Write your Micro-niche.

   ____

Learn more about the same at - https://akhileshtelkar.co.in/

3.5 FINANCIAL POWER

Every individual on this earth wants to earn fast and become financially free.

What is the ultimate meaning here? Can one be called financially free?

ACTIVITY 21

Place one hand on your heart, the other on your mind and say:

"I am ready to make money"

"I am ready to find Passion, Career & Paisa"

"I am ready to become a millionaire"

Being financially free means → ultimately having complete money where earning money is not a problem anymore (it changes from person to person, depending on his desires and requirements).

1. Whatever you are earning or planning to earn and desire, if you attain 25 times your annual income, you can declare yourself of becoming financially free.

   Let's take an example: You want to earn 1 lakh rupees every month, so for a year 12 x 1 = 12 lakhs/annum. Multiply this by twenty-five times that is 25 x 12 = 3 crore - so the day your earnings become 3 crore/annum and if you feel this much money is enough, then you can think of retirement.

2. Another way to think about is - to make assets worth your number amount (paper assets, shares or physical assets) and you get the required interest or rent from those assets. Then this is also typically another way to retire.

3. Assets that can make you financially free are - Mining, Renting, Farming, Real estate, Dividends, Precious metals like Gold, Silver, Business, Social Media, Digital Courses and High-income skills.

3.5.1 Paisa Rules - Money Honey

1. ***Pay yourself first:*** As soon as you get paid, put money in your name like a personal savings account with an auto sweep debit or long-term investment plan.

2. ***Keep a 6-month emergency fund***: Before moving to a new city for a job or changing job or starting a new business - keep a support fund.
3. ***Budget using 40/30/20/10 rule:*** 40% Needs, 30% Want, 20% Investment, 10% Donations.
4. ***Avoid high-interest debt:*** If you have it, use the avalanche or snowball method to payoff (Google for more info).
5. ***When buying a car, use the 30/3/10*** rule if you have to: 30% down, 3 years loan, <10% of your monthly income I still prefer to buy older vehicles with cash.
6. You should save ***15% of your income for retirement.***
7. Have at least ***3 or more times your gross salary in term insurance.***
8. ***Before spending money, wait for 24 hours and ask, do I still want it?*** If you feel so, go ahead and buy. This will save you from a lot of impulse purchases.
9. ***Value time over money*** and experience over things.

Things to Avoid while planning Financials

1. Buying a life insurance policy for investment instead of for protection.
2. Keeping too much money in the savings bank account.
3. Investing only in bank FDs or life insurance policies.
4. Investing in Gold more than 5–10% of your total investment portfolio.

5. Buying a house in a place where one is not sure if he will be working at the same place or will be working at a different place, town or city.
6. Buying vehicles/appliances/furniture, etc. on a loan unless it is absolutely necessary.

3.5.2 Atom age VS Zenit Age

PAST	Future
Work 9-5	Work Anytime
Dependent on the company device	Use any device
Climb corporate ladder	Create your own ladder
Pre-defined Work	Customize Work
Focused on knowledge	Focused on adaptive learning
Office mails	Works on collaboration technologies
Corporate learning and teaching	Democrats learning and teaching

Gone are those days when you were meant to work in 9-5 jobs. Thanks to corona, it has changed the entire prospect of the working-at-home concept.

The above table shows how things have changed and we are heading towards the zenith age.

In the present century, there is a gold mine available in the digital world of social media. It is so vast. We can't imagine right now how the world is changing.

So, if you want to make that gold yours, what are you carrying, a handbag, a trunk, a jeep or a truck?

Best Known will always beat the Best.

Two ways of Business ATOM and BIT:

ATOM	BIT
Physical Business	All Digital presence
Storage, Transport, Distribution	Online, Communication, Digital
Manual interventions	Automation
Always need a physical source	Social Media

Where is the technology heading?

If you are looking at starting a business or joining a company to improve your business, consider the below example.

On October 23, 2001, the Attractive Character of Apple, Steve Jobs, created and launched a new category of digital music players. He stood in front of the world and told everyone that he wanted to revolutionize the music industry (the submarket within which he was building his category). He talked about the other niches within that submarket: a CD would hold 10–15 songs, an MP3 player would hold about 150 songs, and a heavy hard drive would hold about 1,000 songs. And then Steve did something that every leader of every movement throughout time. He did not present them with an "improvement offer" (something that is better, or faster, or almost any word that ends with an "er"). Instead, he created a new category and offered what we call a "new opportunity."

He said that his goal was to make it so that you could put your entire music collection in your pocket and listen to it wherever you go. He then reached into his back pocket and pulled out the first iPod and showed it to the world. This launched his new category, transformed the music industry forever, and made Apple the category king.

As you have seen Apple do this over and over again, it's also true for other companies like Tesla. Elon Musk, the Attractive Character, didn't make a better car; he made an electric car: a new category and a new opportunity. Facebook's Mark Zuckerberg and Google's Larry Page and Sergey Brin did the same in their submarkets. Snapchat's Evan Spiegel and Twitter's Jack Dorsey created a new category and offered a new opportunity. Tony Robbins did it with his personal development content and Russell Brunson with sales funnels. The pattern is repeated over and over again.

Our goal has to be not to fix what's not working. The goal is to replace what's not working with something altogether different.

Most often, when people start thinking about the product or service they want to offer, they start by looking around at what is already out there and try to "build a better on it." When you do that, you are not offering consumers a new opportunity; you are presenting them with an improvement offer. When you create your own category and offer your followers a new opportunity, this gives you a chance to become the category king and have the biggest impact on people's lives.

Rather than trying to improve on someone else's product or service, create a new opportunity to set yourself apart from the competition.

If you want people to buy, you have to show them how your product or service will increase their status.

Status, as I am defining it here, has nothing to do with how other people perceive you, but rather with how you perceive yourself.

Almost every choice in your life has revolved around status—whether you know it or not. For example, what school did you go to? You (or your parents) picked a school because you thought it would elevate your status.

Who did you date? Who did you break up with? Who did you marry? You picked these people and made these choices based on who you thought would elevate your status. What school do your kids go to? What books do you read? What car do you drive? What car do you not drive?

All these things are tied to status. Almost every decision you have ever made was based on this one subconscious question: Is this thing I am considering going to increase my status or decrease it?

When we are looking at any opportunity, we have to decide if it will make us appear smarter, happier, wealthier, more stylish, more powerful, or more attractive. All these things will change our status.

It's only the fear of the unknown, once you learn, it becomes Easy.

NO GUTS NO GLORY

Find "U" in "YOU" is a movement to me.

It's in my birthright to reach out to people and transform their careers.

Nau mahine ki meri kahani tum suno meri jani...
(Listen to my 9 months of story)
Na ata tha na pata tha kuan hai ye Akhilesh
(No one knew who is this Akhilesh)
Social media me to namo nishan na tha
(Did not exist on social media)
Passion meri zindagi me aya...
(Passion came into my life)
Google Karo pata chalege me ab kaun hu meri jani...
(Now Google my name #finduinyou@akhileshtelkar)

As you start on this journey, you will travel through five phases that will help you find your voice, build your tribe, and change the world. Each phase is important in your journey to help impact as many people as possible with your message.

1. Go experiment with a ton of stuff
2. Identify things that spark your interest
3. Engage deeply with those things
4. As you engage, if it goes from interest to true fascination, go down the path of gaining mastery
5. Fascination + Mastery = "Passion, Career & Paisa"

SEE "U" IN "YOU" 1

If we notice people around us, most of them are big Dreamers, but broken in responsibilities. They are more of thinkers and less of doers. Everyone wants to achieve something in life, but when it comes to reality, the fact changes. They will give opinions on everything, but the reality is they have never applied those for themselves. When they see someone throwing garbage on the road, they feel bad about it. If asked what initiative they have taken for the same, they blame the government, people and society. If you are nervous about having what it takes to be a charismatic leader, please read on. My guess is that you are amazing. And I bet that the more amazing you are, the harder it is for you to believe it.

What's common in some best-known success stories?

What's interesting is these amazing people changing the lives of tens of thousands (and in some cases, millions) of people. Almost all of them have an internal pull or want to serve and help people. It's almost like a voice inside them telling them they are destined for greatness.

My results are my Awards, Certifications and this Book.

The new race is born of inner strength

1. Nothing is permanent in this world. Still, we look for a permanent solution, strange but true.
2. Change is constant-
    (i) Change Prime/Netflix with sleep

(ii) Change toxic friends with Mentors

(iii) Change laziness with exercise

(iv) Change negative news with building positive content

3. See the reflection in life-

   (i) Morning rituals without missing

   (ii) Join courses like Vipassana Meditation

   (iii) Write a book and get it published

4. Join a like-minded community.

5. Invest- Invest-Invest...

   The 2022 year alone is an investment year for Self-Development. I have invested more than 5 lakhs to change myself.

6. Read-Read-Read…

   This year, to my surprise, I was able to read 25 books, already watched 100+ videos on self-development, completed courses finished al-read-y... (already). By the time you hold this book, there will be more.

7. Write-Write-Write...

   I never used to write a diary. Now, I have already finished a diary before the year ends, a new diary filled with the best of wisdom.

8. Books-Books-Books…

   Never bought these many books. Now, my shelf looks small...

All credit to my well-wishers who supported me in this journey.

What's your story this year so far?

See "U" in "YOU" 2

If you think you will be successful by doing 10% effort 10 times or 100% effort only one time, it will not give you the result. To go to the success path, the only way is to keep the fire burning all the time, not one time, not twice or ten times, not only on weekends, not daytime or nighttime but to have positive willpower all the time, all the way. Few people start and as time passes, they drop the idea.

This is why only the top 2% of people are successful and the rest are all yet to reach. So know your willpower and live with it. There are chances that when you start your career, you get influenced by many things, friends, relatives and colleagues' advice. You may not be obsessed with the idea you have. You may not want to try one more level or take the risk. So, be careful of the people you chose to validate your ideas. Ensure that they are successful and live a powerful life. Only then you will get the right advice. Otherwise, you will settle for a normal life and end up being common. If you want to do something new and different from the crowd, your thinking also should be like that. When people don't laugh at your ideas, then you are still following the common path, just easygoing and not trying anything great yet.

Regardless of the industry you are in, regardless of the career you choose, and no matter what have been up to, being powerful is mandatory to achieve next-level success.

Ask those who live in bigger cities how they feel about immersion, hundred-hour workweeks, and investing time and money toward growth.

Then find someone obsessed with creating an amazing family. Notice how passionately they talk of family first and love their family. See how dedicated they are to their families.

Talk to an artist or athlete, someone who is obsessed with and constantly improving their particular talent, and see them come alive talking about that thing they do.

You have to embrace this die-trying mentality. There can be no choices and no options. Yes, victory comes at a price—so does settling. Sure, you might be totally and completely insane. But you're not going to stop. Because history shows that only the obsessed make it—people like Alexander the Great, Mother Teresa, Albert Einstein, Barack Obama, Thomas Edison, Elon Musk, Steve Jobs, Charlie Chaplin, Bill Gates, Mark Zuckerberg, Leonardo Di Caprio, Serena Williams, Dr. APJ Abdul Kalam, Narendra Modi and on and on. There is no shortage of these people, and whether we like them or hate them, admire them or detest them, we all know them!

Whether or not you agree with their missions or how they got there, you can't deny that they self-discovered their power—and that's why you know their names. These are people who fought against all odds and were unwilling to settle.

Because they permitted some fanatical, unreasonable, obsessed fascination with their dreams, you and I know their names. Is there a single person we both know the name of who wasn't obsessed? I doubt it.

As you have been reading, you have probably been asking yourself, how do I find what I have?

Maybe you think you already know. Maybe you don't have a clue. Maybe you have lost your way. You could be young and confused or you could be in the midst of a life transition: changing jobs, getting over a relationship, or just done with feeling like you are out of fuel.

I have been there. Throughout my life, for different reasons, I have asked myself these questions again and again:

Why am I doing what I am doing?

What's my purpose?

What is going to get me excited?

When you identify why you want to achieve something, you can fully and completely get obsessed with achieving it. This obsession is what you need to blow away any barriers or opposition you run into on the way to your goal.

What you want from this Life- Find out early, don't be late.

To have what you want in life, you must give yourself permission to throw yourself all in on your career dreams.

Make it clear to others that you are in the urge of finding yourself and becoming a newer person in terms of your career. Though you would like their support, any expectations they may have of your staying where you are, settling for less than you dream, or being average, will have to take a backseat.

Ask yourself, how far up can I go? How much more can I do? And most importantly, what do I want to become completely that makes me a better person who will lead to success?

Being common doesn't take into account your education, your money, or even your abilities.

You will need them eventually, but none of them matters if you haven't first permitted yourself to become a newer version of yourself. It's all about your desire and willingness to see a goal all the way through, despite huge obstacles. Self-discovery saved my life, changed my life, and has given me the life I am living today. It can do the same for you. If I have done one thing right to keep fueling my passion, it has been continuing to invest in my education and development.

Stay hungry, stay safe, and work in a career that drives your passion and brings paisa for you.

Because you picked up this book, I already know you are a big thinker, a big dreamer, and someone who wants to be a huge success.

Good Luck, see you in my webinars or meet you sometime.

Let's See "U" in "YOU" Soon.

Those who love Destination

See "U" in "YOU"

Those who love walking will walk further

SEE "U" IN "YOU" 2

Bonus : 7 Rules for Successful Life

1. **Family First**

   Never forget who was by your side from the start.

   Make time for - your family, friends, partner and children (family comes before your work).

2. **Invest in Yourself**

   Never lose childlike curiosity.

   Be a lifelong learner by - reading books, taking online courses, learning from mentors and experiencing new things (the highest ROI comes from investing in yourself).

3. **Stop comparing yourself**

   Comparison leads to unhappiness - Compete your yesterday with today.

   Focus on - your purpose, your experience, owning your feelings and turning your attention inward.

4. **Find a support system**

   You are the product of your environment.

   Surround yourself with people who are - kind, honest, positive, energetic and supportive. Choose your community wisely.

5. **Be Grateful for what you have**

   Charlie Chaplin once said - I cried because I had no shoes until I met a man who had no food to eat.

   Be thankful for - your life, your job, your home, your family, your health.

   Be grateful for the small things that you have, no matter if it's small or big.

6. **Accept your past and Move on**

   Stop getting stuck in your past, learn from your past to make a better future.

   Life is short, make it sweet.

   Act, Live, Love.

7. **Respect Yourself**

   People learn how to treat you based on how you treat yourself.

   Take action, accept yourself and cut out negative people - you are in control of how you will be treated.

Once a student from a typical middle-class home environment was totally unhappy with whatever he had. He always complained to his parents about not being rich. He was not happy with whatever he had. So, he decided to pray to God and address his complaint.

He jaws, "Oh God, you have given so much money to others, you have given so many amenities to rich people, you have given everything to others, why have you not given me anything?"

God carefully listen to him and checks his records. After a thorough investigation, God notices that most of the time, this person has complaints about people and situations in life. So, He sends Chitragupta to take him to heaven.

Chitragupta reaches the student and says - Chalo (let's go).

The student asks - Where? Who are you?

Chitragupta: Tera time ho gaya, chalo (your time is up, let's go).

Student: Lekin kyun, mujhe nahin ana hai (why, I don't want to come with you).

Chitragupta: Yamraj has sent me here, it's me, Chitragupta.

Student: Hey maharaj, sorry pechchan nahin paya (sorry God! Could not recognize you).

Chitragupta: Theek hai chalo (ok, now let's go).

Student - Kahaan jaana hai (where are we going)?

Chitragupta: Upar - tera hisaab karna hai (to the heaven to check your records).

Student: Parantu muje abhi jeena hai, bhaut kam abhi baki hai (but I still want to live, I have a lot of work to do here).

Chitragupta: No, you complained that you are not happy here, so there is no other option, you have to come with me now.

Student: Meri galti kya hai? Maaf kardo (sorry majesty, forgive me).

Chitragupta: Nahin, tum chalo, upar jaane ke bad pata chalega (no, you will know once you come).

Student (with no option)- Ok.

Chitragupta takes him and drops him in front of a very big lavish bungalow. There were lots of cars parked, a huge door and a lovely balcony. Everything is amazing, the way he wanted.

Student: Wow, it's a beautiful palace, who lives in here?

Chitragupta: It's your house.

Student: Mine, really?

Chitragupta: Ya, you wanted this, right?

Student: Yes, but I never thought that I am so lucky.

Chitragupta smiles.

Student: Are you sure, this big bungalow, swimming pool, garden, cars, lavish interiors sofas, bed, everything is for me only?

Chitragupta nods, hmm.

Student: Wow, maine kabhi socha hi nahin tha ki meri life mein aisa bhi kabhi hoga (I had never thought that my life will turn like this).

The student starts touching everything, everywhere, and says, it's all mine, I am rich now, I have everything.

Chitragupta: Ok enjoy now, I will leave.

In the spell of happiness, the student does not greet Chitragupta properly and says, ok go now, I don't need you.

Chitragupta: Remember one thing - you can call me only once, when it is very urgent.

Student: Ok.

Chitragupta disappears.

The student decides to enjoy each and everything. He goes for a car ride, takes a bath in the lavish bathroom, sits and jumps on the rich fabric sofa, goes to every corner of the room and checks. Then he feels tired and sleeps on the nice cushion bed.

The next day again, he talks to himself, hey see now I do not need my parent's help, no need of friend's support, I am rich now, I can buy anything and can go everywhere.

One more day gets over.

After the 3rd day, he feels the need to talk to somebody. Earlier, he was so blindfolded that he didn't notice if anyone was available around.

This time, he searches, but no one is there.

He then looks for his phone, but there is no phone.

He checks the televisions, radio or any mode of communication - but to no avail.

That night, he feels a little sad. Yet, he is still happy because he has become rich.

Then the next day, again, he starts feeling lonely. So, he goes around to check for people but returns home with disappointment.

On this night, he realizes the complaints he used to make to people around.

Even though he has everything, he can't live happily for long. He understands how badly he treated his parents, relatives and friends. Now he remembers that he can call only once. So, he decides to call Chitragupta.

Student- Sorry my Lord, I thought happiness is in money and becoming rich.

I am a fool that I did not understand all this.

Chitragupta - I hope you don't have complaints about loved ones now!

Student - Yes, I don't want all of these. Whatever I have back at home, I will value.

Health, Relationship and Wealth all are equally important, so value everything.

Earlier, I shared a story about the blue sapphire diamond ring. You might have tried that link (paisa power chapter). Well, it is just a fake link I created. Do not try to see happiness outside. Getting rich quickly by using shortcuts is not a great idea. Value what you have, bring more harmony to your life by finding yourself, See "U" in "YOU" believe and manifest.

"Rivers don't drink their own water,

Trees don't eat their own fruits,

Sun does not shine on itself,

Flowers do not spread fragrance for themselves,

Nature always lives for others selflessly,

We came to his world to serve each other,

No matter how we are,

Life is good when you are happy,

But Life is great when others are happy because of you."

See "U" in "YOU"

— *Akhilesh Telkar*

The Unique Life Guide

The average human spends roughly 79 years or 28,835 days on Earth. So, there are an average of 692,040 hours in a lifetime, would like to spend your most of time doing what you don't like to do? Or you like to follow your passion, build a brand career and make lots of paisa for yourself! The choice is yours.

If you have read this book till here, it shows you are really hungry to change. Many will read this book, but only a few will challenge themselves and will take massive actions.

If you have read and done all the 21 activities - and done more than reading then, "THE UNIQUE LIFE GUIDE IS READY" - You can smile now.

You can get the original copy by filling out this form - https://forms.gle/uu2eVrAFrbnPFP8D9

This book is not only self-experienced but also a practical step-by-step activity laid out to find "U" in "YOU" and success to See "U" in "YOU".

I hope you have understood by now, and might have experienced many parallels in many chapters, but were you able to find your passion? Can you visualize your brand career? How are you going to get the desired paisa for you?

I suggest you to read the book again and do the activities rigorously. I am sure you will see yourself in a different spectrum altogether.

I want to reward you for completing this book. Here is how you can win a free e-Book, free video course, webinar seat, unique guide, career transformation mornings, morning makeup, and write like a pro-30ON30 session for yourself:

Step 1: Share your review of this book on Amazon and Google.

Step 2: Share your key learnings on any social media platform like LinkedIn or Facebook by searching for #finduinyou@akhileshtelkar.

Step 3: Join FB Group -

https://www.facebook.com/groups/3042075812710216/

I am happy that you have now completed this book, but this is not the end. It's the start of your career journey. For more practical help, and one-to-one assistance, reach out to connect@akhileshtelkar.co.in or book a call https://akhileshtelkar.co.in/

In my opinion, with that one book, one course, one person at a time, we can change the world for the better. I ask for your support in making this dream to reality.

Thank you.

Book writing is a creative art; many wish to do, but completing a book requires time, dedication, and brain power, as does any task worth doing.

Here's what I discovered. Out of 97% of people who begin writing a novel: 30 out of 1000 go on to finish it. Only 6 out of those 30 go on to see their book published.

If you are a book lover or an aspirant, who has a quest for a long time to write your book and publish it, then this is for you. Write Like a Pro-30ON30 initiative for book lovers, readers, and writers who need books for their services.

Enroll for the 30ON30 Book Writing Challenge - Complete your long-time quest to become a Best-Selling Author.

What you will get in the 30ON30 Challenge.

1. Private access to Facebook Group WhatsApp group- you will get all my videos here
2. Recorded session on How to write an E-book
3. Daily, I will share How to embark on your journey toward becoming Author
4. All your doubts, challenges, and difficulties - get addressed in 1:1 calls
5. Thirty Secrets to Write like a Pro
6. Morning Prayers, Gratitude, Affirmations
7. Daily reading and writing practice
8. Self-Publish support
9. Marketing support
10. Career Clarity
11. Morning Mind Makeup
12. Story Telling Sessions
13. Author's Voice
14. Podcast

Not only this, there are lots of surprises and good news. You can take advantage of the opportunity to create a new version of your writing journey-

Connect for more details: https://akhileshtelkar.co.in/

ABOUT THE AUTHOR

Akhilesh Telkar is an Indian author who has written Find "U" in "YOU" and See "U" in "YOU" He has been recognised for his work "Best Excellence Award" during his career because his dad left when he was eight years old, his mother becomes everything to him.

16-20 > Struggler,

20-30 > Soldier,

30-40 > Hunter

At the beginning of his career, he had 10Rs meals a day, and now after a year's experience in the corporate world, becoming an author was challenging. However, the author says the world has many opportunities; we must listen to our inner voice.

As he gained experience and technology skills, he developed a passion for "Writing." (Passion + Tech = Passiontech)

However, one question always bothered him,

"What is one thing you want to leave behind for the world?"

At that moment, "BOOK" occurs to him as a guiding torch, a document that will remain even after we leave this world.

The good news is that he develops the Find "U" in the "YOU" framework in the self-discovery journey.

And the book, See "U" in "YOU", based on the topic "Passion, Career & Paisa", the Unique life Guide, has 21 activities.

Let us create a world full of love, joy and happiness. Thank you, Cheers,

Akhilesh quotes:

I can adapt quickly to any situation

I am a loyal follower

I am a good listener

I believe in change and am a creative thinker

"Rasta mushkil ho, (The path may be difficult)

Mansil ki doori ka pata na ho, (Clueless about the distance to the destination)

Jab saath kudrath ho, (When the universe is with us)

Kathin kaam bi aasan ho." (Even hard work becomes easy)

Akhilesh Dream is to live in a world of beautiful people where everyone understands each other and finds themselves by seeing "U in YOU" live a happy life.

On Mission To Unlock Human Potential Through Creative Books | Author | Mentor For Writers | Framework Find "U" in "YOU" | Unique Life Guide Creator of See "U" in "YOU" | HashtagKalakar | Passion Tech Mentor | Content Writer | Ghost Writer| Passion, Career & Paisa | Passionprenuer

Vision: To unlock your potential & reap success in your Life".

Mission: To touch the hearts of 10M readers to transform & help them to grow and build a life with passionate dreams

Akhilesh Telkar, *Author*

https://linktr.ee/akhi.ts

ANSWERS FOR THE TREE EXERCISE

1. Optical illusions are a hot trend these days, and it seems the internet's appetite for having its collective mind boggle and bent is stronger than ever.
2. A total of 10 National Leaders are in that Tree, the artwork named 'National Leaders Tree'.

According to the artist, the faces spotted are Rajiv Gandhi, Indira Gandhi, Rabindra Nath Tagore, Subhash Chandra Bose, Mahatma Gandhi, Lal Bahadur Shastri, Jawar Lal Nehru, Gopal Krishna Gokhale, Chandrashekar Azad and Dr. Radhakrishnan.

Why has this exercise been shared?

The first reason behind selecting this tree is to give due respect to the artist - I want everyone to think out of the box and become creative.

The second reason is that these are great life-changing leaders. We should take inspiration from them while we are on our way to achieving our goals in life.

Sath do din ka tha (There are a few days of life)
Lekin safar zindagi hai (The journey is about living)
Dost bohut honge (Friends may be many)
Lekin hum jaise kum hi hoge (Like me may be few)
Yuhi chalthe raho sath sath... (Let's go and grow together)
Manzil kushiyon ki taraf badhte raho sath sath...
(Reach success, happiness together)

Everyone has a story to tell, everyone is a walking book
Action is all that remains - that's penning it down
Next, let's See "U" in "YOU".

Passion, Career & Paisa

The Only difference between your

Past "U" and Present "YOU"

See "U" in "YOU"

ALL IN ONE CONNECT

https://linktr.ee/akhi.ts

SCAN QR CODE

Find "U" in "You"
AKHILESH TELKAR
KNOW YOUR POTENTIAL
CHANGE THE OLD BELIEF
REAP THE SUCCESS
kindle

Write Like a Pro
30ON30 Secrets